MANUAL
OF GRAPHIC TECHNIQUES 4
FOR ARCHITECTS, GRAPHIC DESIGNERS, & ARTISTS
TOM PORTER AND SUE GOODMAN

Charles Scribner's Sons · New York

Acknowledgments

The authors would like to thank the following people for their help in providing material and information for the production of this manual:

    Simon Barton, Johnny Cadell, Kong Tak Cheung, Sonny Ching, Roger Cumming, Jack Forman, Martin Gordon, Ron Hess, Nigel Hiscock, David Koh, Mike Leech, Stuart Lewis, Gordon Nelson, and Catherine Tramner.

Special thanks are also due to Iradj Parvaneh and Ivor Fields for all photography, and to Pat McNiff for typing the text.

Library of Congress Cataloging in Publication Data

Porter, Tom.

   Manual of graphic techniques 4.

   1. Graphic arts--Technique. I. Goodman, Sue.
II. Title.
NC1000.P684 1985   741.6   85-50242
ISBN 0-684-18216-5

1 3 5 7 9 11 13 15 17 19   Q/P   20 18 16 14 12 10 8 6 4 2

Printed in the United States of America.

TABLE
OF CONTENTS

Introduction

Manual of Graphic Techniques 4 has been developed specifically as a companion and concluding volume to its forerunners in the series, Manual of Graphic Techniques 1, 2, and 3. Based on the now familiar format of self-contained page layouts and step-by-step frames of information, its intention is to introduce the beginning design student to a deeper understanding of the basic range of graphic systems and their use in design.

When a design concept is transferred initially from the space of a designer's thought processes into an externalized form, any one of a basic range of drawing systems may be called upon to give graphic birth to the idea. Similarly, when a three-dimensional concept is evolved along the ensuing design sequence, it may be identified, examined, tested, and finally communicated to others using the same range of representational vehicles. It is to this basic set of design tools that this manual turns.

The first three chapters deal with the plan, elevation, and the section, respectively. These are "two-dimensional" orthographic views that represent a series of different but penetrating views of a designed form in which each supplements the information not given in the others. However, when used as a set they collectively provide a complete three-dimensional explanation of the form under study. As the plan, elevation, and section do not rely upon perspective depth, each drawing mode is presented with its potential for conversion, via available depth cues, into a more pictorial appearance. The orthographic conventions are also explained together with drafting methods and rendering techniques appropriate to each type of drawing.

The family of orthographic projection drawings known as axonometrics and isometrics is the subject of Chapter 4. These are often referred to as "three-dimensional drawings" but, although simulating a depth illusion, they do not rely upon perspective convergence for this impression. In functioning as graphic containers for a single view that combines the plan, elevation, or section, metric projection drawings usually appear in the design process to test an evolving idea "in the round." They are also widely used to communicate the preview of a design proposal to others. The range of bird's-eye and worm's-eye viewpoints inherent in this drawing genre are presented, together with the various drafting methods and rendering techniques.

The fifth and final chapter deals with perspective, the one means of graphic representation that comes closest to our perception of space. Here, an office method of constructing two-point perspectives is explained together with some hints and tips for improving perspective drawings destined for use in presentation. Also included is a number of unusual methods for producing perspective illusions of designs seemingly occupying the space of their intended settings.

1 PLANS

Introducing Orthographic Projection

Historically, an air of mystery seems to have always surrounded the drawing techniques of architects and designers. For instance, little is known about the graphic techniques of designers in the Middle Ages. This may be due to the fact that, together with the secrecy surrounding building methods used in the erection of Gothic cathedrals, knowledge of the state of the art remained firmly locked within the confines of a medieval guild membership. In fact, one medieval architect is known to have assassinated his bishop client in order to protect those secrets from inquisitive eyes. So, too, during the Italian Renaissance one of the inventors of perspective, Filippo Brunelleschi, was heard to remark, "Do not share your inventions with many." Therefore, it comes as no surprise that when the eighteenth century military engineer Gaspard Monge devised a method of orthographic projection drawing that simplified the graphic understanding of more complicated forms, his method became immediately classified as "top secret" government information. However, his method of projection drawing that allows a mapping of a standardized relationship between the plan, side, and front views of an object soon became the common currency of both engineering and architectural drawing.

Monge's method is known as "first angle projection." The best way of visualizing it is to imagine an object "boxed" by a three-sided container.

1 2

The significant faces of the contained object are projected as straight parallel lines directly onto the inside planes of the cubic conceptual box.

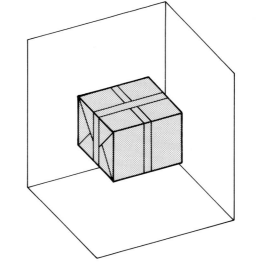
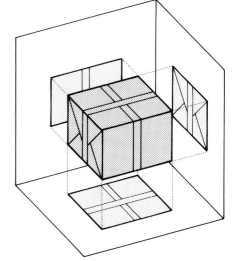

When the container is opened out, a separate view is obtained from each of the object's faces--the number of views corresponding to the amount of information required to fully describe the object. The unfolded series of images provides a complete picture of the object under study, the inner surfaces of the box becoming the drawing surface, or the picture plane.

N.B.: If we replace the object with an image of a building we can see how important this system of projection is to architectural design and communication.

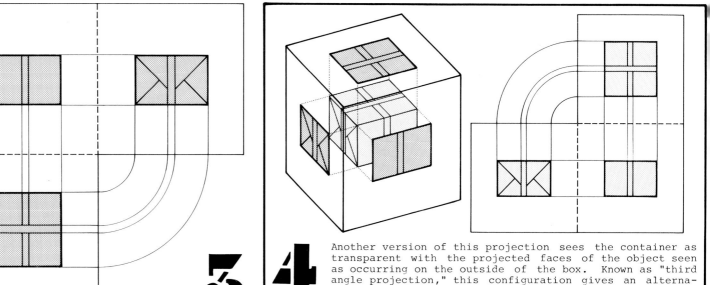

3 4

Another version of this projection sees the container as transparent with the projected faces of the object seen as occurring on the outside of the box. Known as "third angle projection," this configuration gives an alternative orthographic layout when the box is opened flat.

The Plan, Elevation, and Section

1 The plan, elevation, and section represent our conceptual movement about the space occupied by an object or a building. Each drawing type reflects a vantage point from which the designer can examine an invented form that is either visualized in the mental space of an idea or recorded in the multi-facets of a three-dimensional existence in real space. For example, the plan takes us on a graphic journey above the form, while the elevation takes us around its sides at ground level. Meanwhile, after cutting away a slice from the form, the section invites us inside for a scrutiny of its internal workings.

2

Within this orthographic sequence, the scale and proportion of each drawing mode remains constant in all dimensions. This allows the spatial and dimensioned information to be transferable, with each drawing supplementing the information missing from the others. The information is then repackaged and presented together to provide a complete picture of even the most complicated architectural forms.

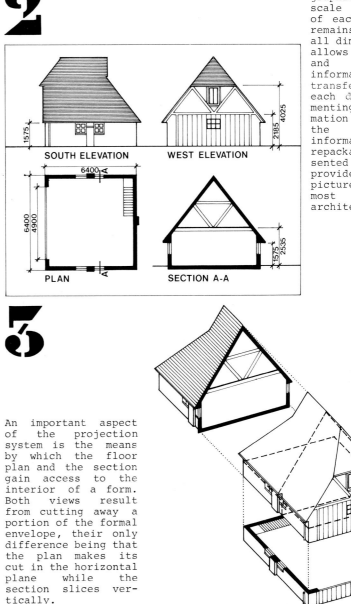

SOUTH ELEVATION   WEST ELEVATION

PLAN   SECTION A-A

3

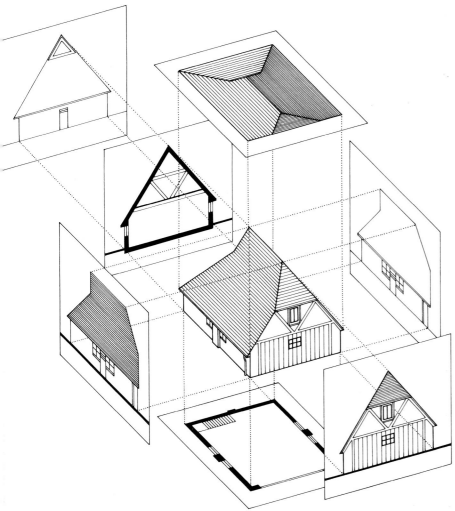

An important aspect of the projection system is the means by which the floor plan and the section gain access to the interior of a form. Both views result from cutting away a portion of the formal envelope, their only difference being that the plan makes its cut in the horizontal plane while the section slices vertically.

Scale in Plans

1

Plans can be used to represent formal events as small as a child's toy and as large as a city. Therefore, the size of a drawing in relation to what it attempts to communicate is important. For example, the plan of the toy can be shown at same-size, i.e., one-to-one, while in order to accommodate its extent on a sheet of paper the city plan has to be drastically shrunk conceptually and drawn to a scale of 1 : 12,500.

N.B.: When detailing an architectural design, it is wise never to draw elements at half-size (1 : 2) because a builder may misread this scale as full-size.

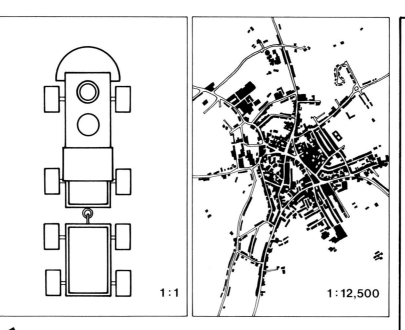

1:1

1:12,500

2

Therefore, the selection of scale for an orthographic drawing is a means of regulating the distance between the designer's eye (or mind's eye) and the size or degree of complexity of an object or a concept.

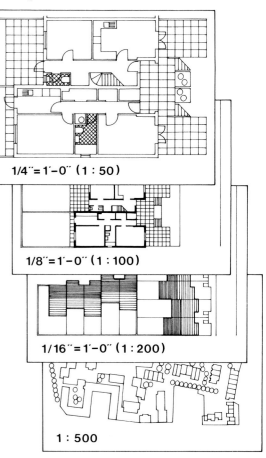

1/4″=1′-0″ (1 : 50)

1/8″=1′-0″ (1 : 100)

1/16″=1′-0″ (1 : 200)

1 : 500

In building design, floor plans are usually drawn at 1/4″ = 1′-0″ (1 : 50) or 1/8″ = 1′-0″ (1 : 100). Increasingly larger buildings and building complexes can be shrunk along decreasing scales of 1/16″ = 1′-0″ (1 : 200) or 1 : 500.

3

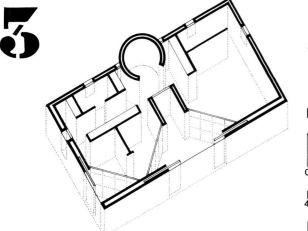

In its role as a horizontal section, the floor plan is usually sliced around 5′-0″ (1500mm) above the ground-plane. This is so that the location of openings, especially those of windows and doors, can be recorded along the trajectory of the cut.

4

The graphic representation of a scale tends to be used with the plan only when the resultant drawing is to be resized graphically. However, whenever a drawn scale is used, its proportional units of linear measurement should be clearly and simply indicated.

IMPERIAL SCALES

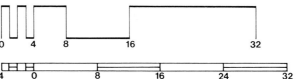

0   4   8   16   32

4 0   8   16   24   32

METRIC SCALES

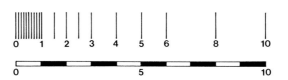

0 1 2 3 4 5 6   8   10

0   5   10

Floor and Ceiling Plans

1 When describing multi-level buildings, a series of floor plans may be used, such as shown here by this stack of floor plans taken from a house design by le Corbusier.

N.B.: The ground floor plan often extends itself out to include floorscape and landscape treatments that occur beyond the area occupied by the building plan. Less common is the inclusion of the roof plan except in smaller-scale site plans or, as in this case, when it has something special to say.

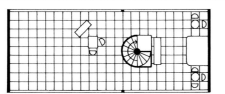

ROOF PLAN

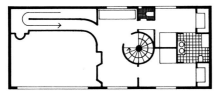

THIRD FLOOR

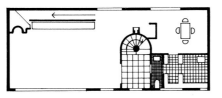

SECOND FLOOR

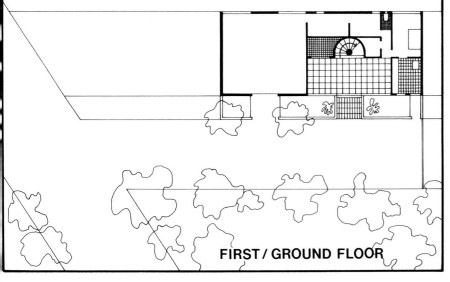

FIRST / GROUND FLOOR

Plans of ceilings are the least common of plan views. When presented they describe distinctive features, such as exposed runs of lighting or ducting. Two types are in orthographic currency, one of which depicts this plane as seen from below. When used this version is for presentation only and is never used for communicating with a builder. The more useful mirrored, or reflected version flips this plane laterally so that its information matches that of its accompanying floor plan.

2

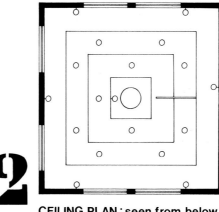

CEILING PLAN: seen from below

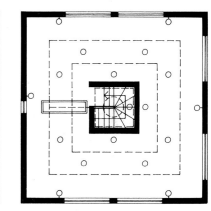

REFLECTED CEILING PLAN

An important distinction in orthographics is the difference between design drawings and working, or production drawings. Design drawings tend to be concerned with the appearance of a building to the client, while production drawings describe precise constructional information and are aimed at the builder.

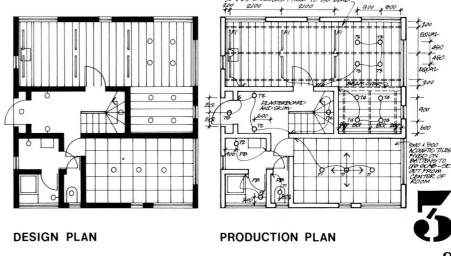

DESIGN PLAN

PRODUCTION PLAN

3

Line Quality and Convention

As the use of line lies at the heart of architectural drafting, it is important to consider some of its qualities and conventions. Line quality can be classified into three basic categories. The first appears in drawings that exclusively employ lines of equal weight. Even-weight line drawings can appear precise and sharp but, when drafted insensitively, can appear as "wooden" or lifeless graphics.

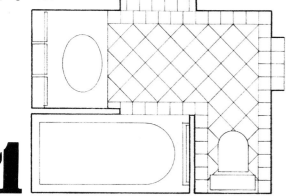

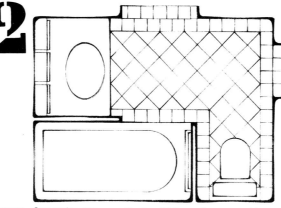

A more dynamic type of drafting is one that transforms a line from thick-to-thin-to-thick along its length. By varying its thickness and intensity, this line type seems stretched and in tension, and appears to embody a "life" of its own. Also, the end-of-line pressure ensures an unambiguous line that makes a positive contact with others in the drawing.

The thick-to-thin line is achieved by sensing its "elasticity" during drafting. When drawing such lines designers will often rotate the pencil between forefinger and thumb at an angle of 45-degrees--this drawing action helping to retain a sharpened pencil point.

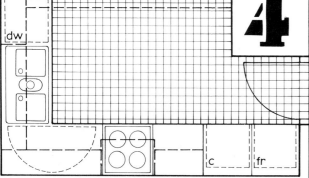

The dashed or broken line represents the third category. This line has an important function in orthographics because it represents a convention of depth. For instance, lines that are broken using short dashes function as "hidden lines" and signify objects that occur behind the plane of the drawing. Conversely, long-dashed lines signify objects that occur forward of the plane, i.e., between the viewer and the cut.

By exploiting line quality and line weight the abstraction of plans can take on an implied spatial existence. For example, a descending scale of line thickness and weight that corresponds to a decreasing scale of planar depth (or degrees of importance of information) will create the depth illusion.

N.B.: As part of this hierarchy, the graphic treatment of the plan cut should always exist as the most prominent feature.

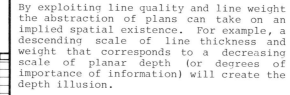

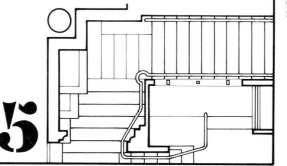

The drawings of many well-known architects display distinctive drafting styles that have been fine-tuned as vehicles for the evolution and communication of design concepts. Therefore the development of a personal drawing technique that is both responsive and expressive is important. This is because our more adventurous visualizations are always in danger of being imprisoned within the limitations of an inadequate or insensitive graphic language. The design sketches illustrated here are based on the work of Michael Graves.

Line Weights and Value Scales

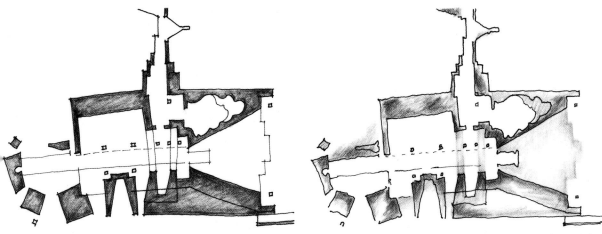

2 Line weights can be translated basically into grades of graphite and into technical pen nib sizes. Furthermore, various line thickness or, particularly with pencils, variation in pressure of application, can be assigned to some of the specific drafting conventions.

NIB SIZE		PENCIL
0.5mm	Outline of cut	B
0.35mm	Lines inside the plan	HB
0.25mm	Hidden lines	H OR 2H
0.18mm	Dimension lines	4H
0.18mm	Section lines	4H

N.B.: Remember that too much pressure on the harder graphite grades will cause grooves in the drawing material.

1 The use of a drafting technique that enlists an expressive line quality and a breadth of line weight is the first step in the development of a personal graphic style. As part of this development, line weight should correspond directly to a creative thinking process that emphasizes "nearer" or important planes and points. For example, here are two sketch plans, each with a subtly different emphasis. The one on the left concentrates on an emphasis of form by defining the cut through the plan, while the one on the right (after Michael Graves) shifts its emphasis to the space as defined by the cut.

Within this prioritization of plan information, the rendering of the cut remains the paramount element in the drawing. Depending on scale, medium, and required intensity, the cut can be contrasted by a heavy delineation, rendered as solid black, or be picked out in a halftone via pencil shading, pen hatching, or by using markers, ink or watercolor wash, or dry-transfer screens.

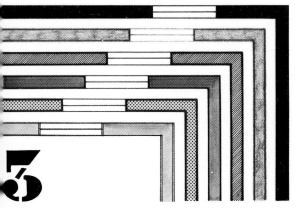

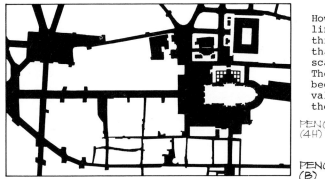

4 Another means of increasing the plan's spatial capacity is to reverse the traditional roles of medium and paper. Although usually reversed by reprographic techniques, the representation of "positive" or "solid" by white against the representation of "negative" or "void" by black is useful for gaining an increased spatial insight to the relationship of "container" and "contained," especially in urban site plans.

5 However, the spatial implication of line-drawn plans is further extended through descending scales of value that are applied to corresponding scales of depth in multilevel plans. Therefore, it is important for the beginner to experience calibrated value scales by experimenting with the various tone-giving mediums.

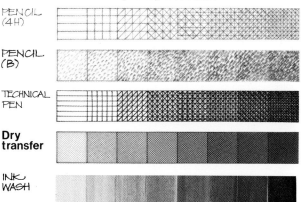

PENCIL (4H)

PENCIL (B)

TECHNICAL PEN

Dry transfer

INK WASH

Drafting the Plan

1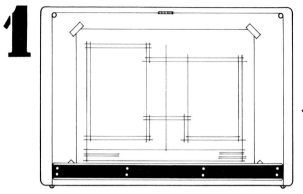

When setting-out the plan, begin by drafting its main outlines, making sure that its layout is either centered on the sheet or located so that sufficient space remains for any additional graphics, titles, and so on.

N.B.: Decisions regarding the scale at which to depict the plan will depend on the full-size dimensions of the building in mind, the level of detail you wish to convey, and the size of the drawing board.

2 A preliminary construction drawing should be first worked in faint pencil lines. The framework of its main outlines should be plotted around fixed reference points. For example, significant structural points, such as columns, or known linear elements, such as existing site walls.

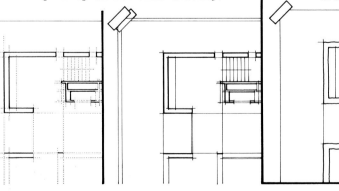

3 Grids provide a useful device on which to hang the primary and secondary lines of construction in plans, especially when the design involves a modular structural system. When using transparent drawing material, graph paper can be placed underneath the sheet as a direct drafting aid.

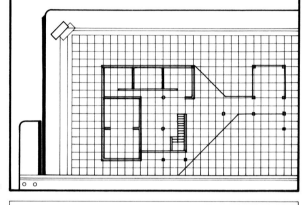

4 A method of avoiding the erasure of drafting errors is to first work the plan in blue non-repro pencil on tracing paper. This is then selectively overworked in pen--the ink line only being printed by diazo reproduction. Another method is to work the preparatory drawing in pencil on paper before overlaying with tracing paper to selectively extract the final plan by an ink line tracing.

5 An excellent method of avoiding the sterile appearance of totally mechanically drawn plans is to overwork the pencil construction drawing with a freehand ink line. In this technique the apparently spontaneous quality of its freehand lines is harnessed by the dimensional accuracy of the under-drawing.

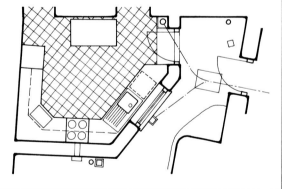

6 Finally, the application of all primary and supportive linear information can be beefed up by using line weight variation to stretch the illusion of the third dimension. Also, a use of the thin-to-thick line technique will help to fix in a positive manner all the corners and the points of connection that are critical to the plan.

Plan Symbols: Openings and Staircases

The degree of detail used when representing any architectural element in orthographics is dependant on the scale at which it is depicted, a common error being the attempt to illustrate too much detail at the smaller scales or too little at the larger scales. These examples show typical conventional plan symbols for doors, windows, and staircases with some indication of the level of detail appropriate to the various scales.

DOORS

1/16" TO 1'0" (1:200)

1/8" TO 1'0" (1:100)

1/4" TO 1'0" (1:50)

1/2" TO 1'0" (1:20)

SINGLE LEAF SINGLE ACTION
DOUBLE LEAF SINGLE ACTION

SINGLE LEAF DOUBLE ACTION
REVOLVING DOOR

FOLDING DOOR CENTER HUNG
FOLDING DOOR EDGE HUNG

SLIDING DOOR HUNG IN RECESS
SLIDING DOOR FACE HUNG

The swing door is indicated by a single or double line at right angles to the wall, and the swing of its opening edge denoted by a quadrant or semicircle. Occasionally, designers will indicate the swing with a diagonal line but, as this does not describe the path of the swing, it appears as a less elegant symbol.

WINDOWS

1/16" TO 1'0" (1:200)

1/8" TO 1'0" (1:100)

1/4" TO 1'0" (1:50)

1/2" TO 1'0" (1:20)

SIDE HUNG OPENING LIGHTS

N.B.: Much more information on window type is gained from the elevation drawing. In elevation a simple convention of diagonal lines explains the direction of opening lights as seen from outside the building.

LEFT-HAND HUNG CASEMENT

RIGHT-HAND HUNG CASEMENT

VERTICAL SLIDING SASH

TOP HUNG CASEMENT

BOTTOM HUNG CASEMENT

VERTICAL PIVOT

HORIZONTAL PIVOT

HORIZONTAL SLIDING SASH

STAIRCASES

DOG-LEG OR U-TYPE STAIRCASE

1/4" TO 1'0" (1:50)

1/16" TO 1'0" (1:200)   1/8" TO 1'0" (1:100)

STRAIGHT FLIGHT

RAMP

SPIRAL STAIRCASE

ELEVATOR

Arrows should always indicate "up" on staircases and ramps. This is because the two-way marking of "up" and "dn" produces a confusing palindrome. A broken diagonal line is used to cut the point at which a flight of stairs passes through the information contained in the plan. Notice that as scale increases, more detailed information may be included.

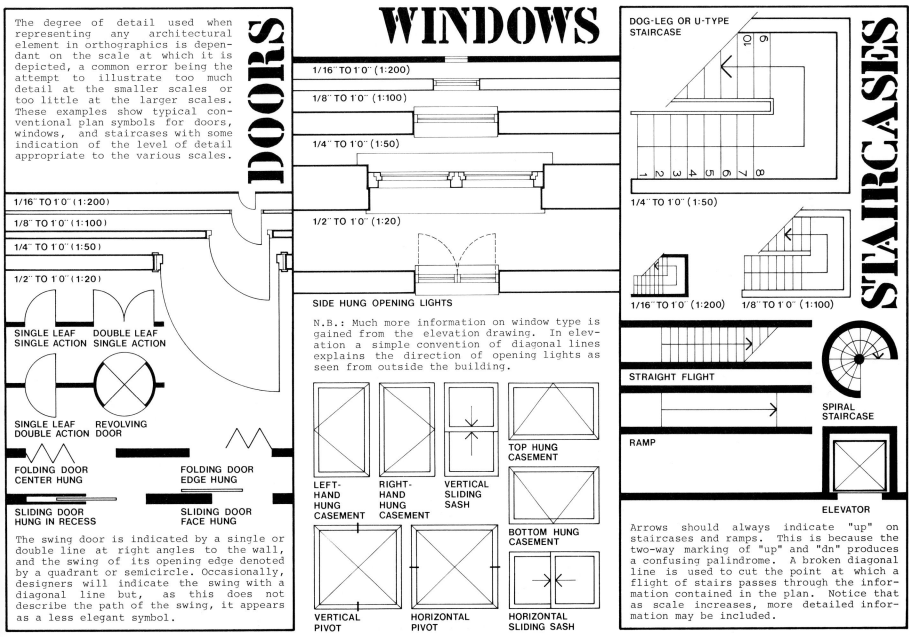

The Interior Plan

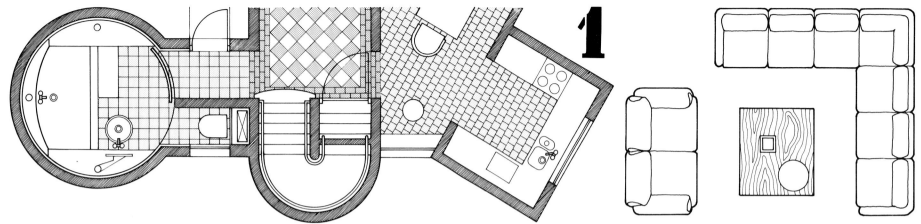

1

Interior plans are used by interior designers and architects to illustrate the intent of an interior design. When combined with a diagrammatic but positive graphic cut through the thicknesses of walls, the contained space tends to be rendered in a pictorial manner. This is because such plans often concentrate on the patterns and colors of floor finishes, coverings, furniture, and fittings. In so doing, the interior plan becomes an invaluable vehicle for detailed design because, being drawn to the larger scales of 1/2" = 1' (1 : 20) and 1/4 = 1' (1 : 50), it studies the feasibility of habitable space in terms of layout, circulation, and the working relationship between fixed objects and those independent of the structure.

2

As badly drawn or rendered furniture and fittings will appear to contaminate the clear impression of space necessary to this graphic, keep the drawing of such elements as simple as possible. When in doubt, modify known examples or use the graphic conventions (see facing page).

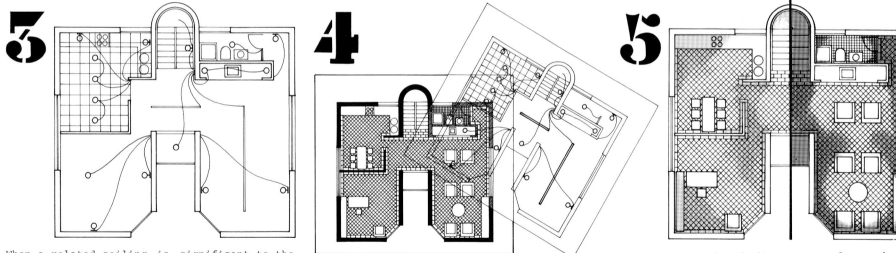

3

When a related ceiling is significant to the design, a reflected ceiling plan, i.e., a mirrored plan that coincides with the floor plan, may be imposed directly on less elaborated interior plans using the accepted convention.

4

Otherwise, the planned location of ceiling modules, ducting, illuminaires, lighting tracks, and so on, should be shown alongside the floor plan, or superimposed over it as a transparent overlay.

5

The indication by shading or a color wash of sunlight as it penetrates interiors is another opportunity of pictorializing interior plans. Alternatively, an after-dark impression of specialized electric lighting effects can be shown.

Plan Symbols: Furniture and Fittings

1 The larger scales of interior floor plans allow some scope for the graphic description of surface finishes. For instance, in furniture layouts the sensitive use of markers, colored pencils, or watercolor washes inside a simple outline drawing can, apart from indicate color and texture, also hint at form. Furthermore, a discrimination between surface materials, such as wood, plastic, stone, and fabrics can be suggested by subtle hatching.

CHAIRS

TABLES

CUPBOARDS AND CABINETS

BEDS AND BATHROOM FURNITURE

KITCHEN FITTINGS AND WORKTOPS

N.B.: As mentioned previously, modify known examples of furniture. The chairs on this page represent some of the classics. Can you recognize them?

2

The alternative to drawing your own symbols is to use the vast range of custom templates and dry-transfer materials that, being manufactured at different scales, aid the rapid insertion of architectural symbols into orthographics. Although these will prove a useful expedient to the designer in a hurry, their use should not deny experiments that aim to integrate a representation of such elements into the overall graphic quality of larger-scale plans.

The Site Location Plan and the Site Plan

1

Location plans and site plans are key drawings in the set of orthographics used to present building designs. This is because they orientate the viewer by offering an introductory overview of the nature of both the wider context and the immediate setting of a proposed building. For instance, a location plan may be used at a scale that illustrates the city, state, county, or regional context and demonstrates transportation links, distances, and travel times within the territory covered by the plan.

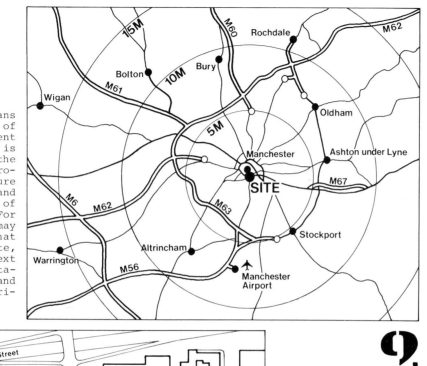

3

A site plan again zooms our view up in scale to a concentration on the site area itself. Usually drafted at scales of 1/16" = 1' (1 : 200), or 1 : 500, and sometimes at 1 : 2500, site plans depict the surrounding terrain of a proposed building.

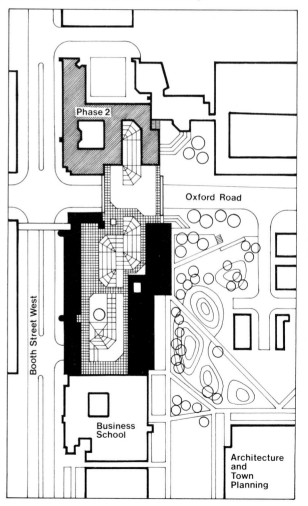

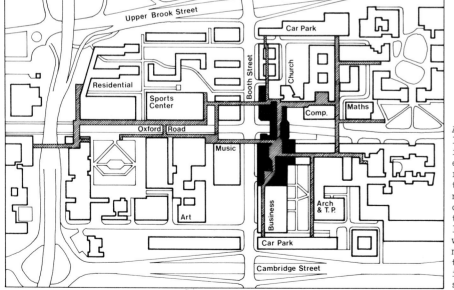

2

Another version of the location plan zooms into a larger-scale examination of the relationship between the site and its neighborhood. In this contextual view, local transport and utility links, zoning, together with any related or major architectural or topographical features in the locality, may be shown.

The Site Plan

1 When a proposed building is designed for a rural setting, the site plan usually illustrates the natural physical topography of the terrain including land undulation, walkways, driveways, trees, landscaping, boundaries, and any watercourses, etc. Using simple linear conventions, these elements can all be drafted with a minimum of fuss.

N.B.: A site plan will occasionally be presented minus its design proposal, i.e., to depict the location of existing site features prior to design. However, when the building plan is included it is wise to show all modifications to the landscape as they would appear in a mature state.

2 If the setting for a building design is urban, the site plan will describe the proximity of existing and adjacent architectural form together with other man-made or natural elements that will have impact on the intended building.

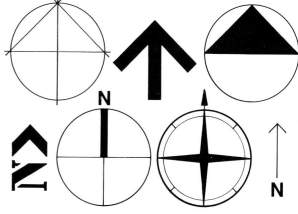

N.B.: Site plans usually turn out to be of a larger scale than the remainder of the drawings in a set of orthographics. However, they can be reduced proportionally to maintain a continuity of format.

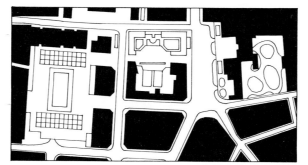

4 The first known site plan is of a layout for a tamarisk grove fronting an Eleventh Dynasty temple at El-Dier el-Bahari in Memphis, Egypt. Drawn in 2100 B.C., this plan also displays the first recorded "architectural" error as the layout strays over the site limits—a mistake that was later crudely erased by its designer.

3 A convention in site plans is that they are drafted with north occurring at the top of the drawing. North points should be positioned clearly on the plan, their design being the prerogative of the designer. Here are some unambiguous examples of north points.

Therefore, it is important that confusion is avoided by delineating clearly the limits of a site area. Boundaries are usually indicated using the convention of a broken or a dotted line, or even delineated in color.

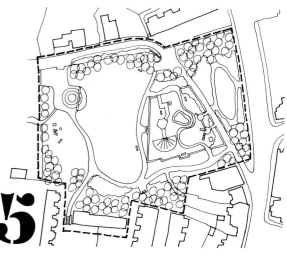

5

17

The Convention of Contours

1 Contour lines in site plans are a graphic convention for describing changes in level in the surface of landscape. Contours represent imaginary lines that symbolize a constant height above sea level or another reference datum and trace the elevation of that height in a continuous manner.

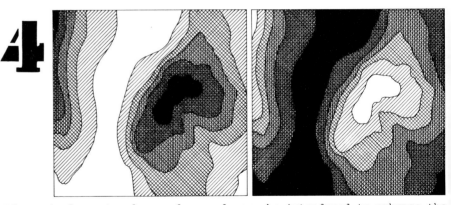

2

A good way of visualizing contour lines is to imagine that the landform is sliced through horizontally at regularly calibrated intervals --evidence of each cut being represented by the line of the contour. The choice of calibration for the set distance between the points at which the contours are given depends on the scale of the plan, and is expressed in feet or meters. Contours on larger scale site plans are usually spaced at intervals of 2', 4', or 6' (0.5M, 1M, or 2M), but other intervals can be used.

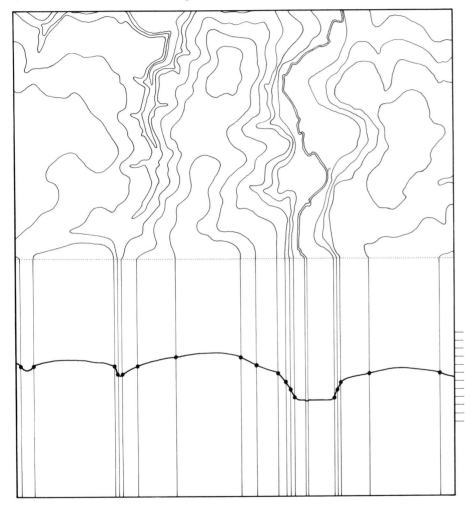

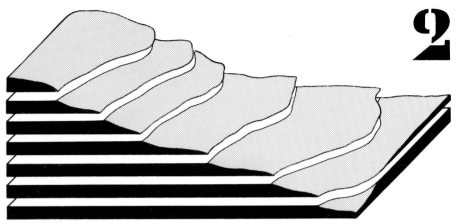

4

If required, a tonal or color scale can be introduced to enhance the depth information of contour plans. Stepped progressions of value can either ascend or descend the altitude of the contours as both interpretations of this scale appear to convey a three-dimensional illusion. Rendering mediums for contours include the airbrush or aerosol color spray--either using a system of progressive masking. Other methods include watercolor washes, dry-transfer tones, colored pencil, or pen or pencil hatching. Watercolor and spray color washes are quickly built up over a total initial wash, successive washes of the same medium and intensity progressively excluding each contour in turn as they ascend or descend the altitude of the plan.

3 When reading contour plans, the trajectory of each line informs on the shape of the land formation at that elevation. The distance between each line indicates the degree of undulation of the site. For example, contour lines that are close together indicate a steep rise in elevation. If they are far apart, the terrain is relatively flat.

Contextual Roof Plans and Floor Plans

When site plans function as the context for a building design the possibility exists of a pictorial treatment that can convert the abstraction of the plan into an image approaching the reality of an aerial view. This kind of figurative orthographic is important when communicating with clients and laypersons as it is closer to their understanding of form and space than the diagrammatic data of a raw orthographic.

In smaller-scale site plans buildings are generally shown as a roof plan. This drawing then concentrates on an elaboration of the physical features of the surrounding site space. When shadows are cast in such drawings, a positive-negative illusion is obtained that allows "upright" objects, such as trees and buildings, to be judged as elements occupying space (see page 22). This drawing is based on a detail of a site plan by Trevor Horne.

1

However, when the site plan scale coincides with that of the larger scales of other drawings in the presentation, the architectural form is often cut away to expose the first floor plan. If drafting time permits, this type of graphic is extremely useful in both design detailing and communication as it provides a spatial continuum that--via openings and transitional spaces--connects "inside" with "outside." Relationships between the modular texture of interior floorscape finishes can then be compared simultaneously with the grain of exterior paving and site groundscaping. Also, interior planting may be seen as an extension of site landscaping. Furthermore, shadows may be cast to enhance the depth illusion of contours but, unlike those cast from roof plans, shadows from first floor plans are--when shown--cast to the height of the cut, i.e., approximately 4' (1200mm). This drawing is based on the work of Robert Stern.

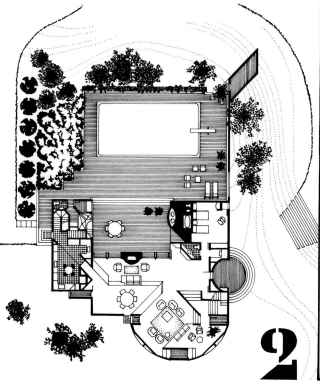

2

3 This is a detail based on a pen-drawn plan of Ralph Erskine's house designed in 1941. The building plan is shown as an integral facet of the terraced landscape and, together with his rich expression of a variegated groundscape, celebrates his love for nature. The drawing is literally packed with surface detailing including a graphic discrimination between deciduous and evergreen trees.

Drawing Trees and Shrubs

Trees in plan can be categorized into two basic types of view: overhead view--with the texture of foliage being deployed in response to the direction of sunlight in order to suggest their canopy; and sectional view--in which the slice, either with or without foliage, exposes both trunk and branches. Drafting begins with a guideline circle around a central point, designers developing their own personal style along degrees of abstraction but always with the amount of detail corresponding to the scale and purpose of the plan. Also, trees can be shown to cast shadows and, especially when information needs to be shown below their canopy, they can become extremely simplified to allow an X-ray view.

Shrubbery and hedging is usually delineated with a thinner line, especially when shown in the proximity of trees. Furthermore, as shrubs are usually landscaped in groups, one containing outline can describe the mass of a cluster of individual plants.

20

Rendering Groundcover and Floorscape

1 There are several basic pencil and pen techniques for simulating grass in site plans. These include the pointilliste effect of clustered dots, either hand-drawn or sprayed within a mask; clusters of line-flecks, either ordered into layers, structured by contours, or freely deployed; and a texture produced by layers of organized "scribble." Other effects are rapidly achieved by inserting a glasspaper underlay beneath the plan for the purpose of taking a direct graphite "rubbing." When grass simulation moves to larger scale plans, the more laborious techniques can be economized by their concentration around the periphery of a grassed area to suggest the whole, be localized in corners, or be confined to the double-function of depicting shadows.

2 In larger-scale floor plans and site plans, a delineated description of floorscape treatments can inform the viewer about the progression and pattern of floor finishes connecting interior and exterior space. Floorscape is usually shown as a simplified version of its aerial appearance but should always recognize a constructional relationship with the building plan. In other words, modular floor units should be shown in a manner that is responsive to the reality of their actual installation.

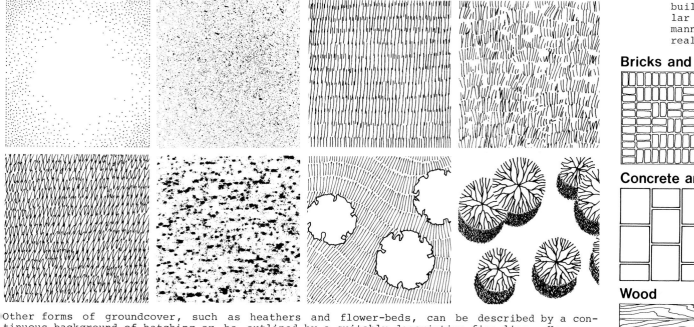

Other forms of groundcover, such as heathers and flower-beds, can be described by a continuous background of hatching or be outlined by a suitably descriptive fine line. However, degree of detail and density of effect must not intimidate the impact of formal events, such as trees, that appear above the groundplane.

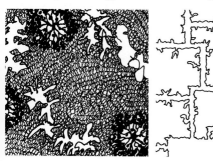

Bricks and Brick Paviors

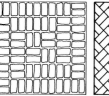
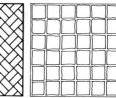

Concrete and Stone Paving

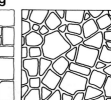

Wood

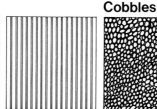

Cobbles

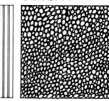

Water

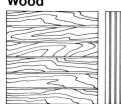

Gravel

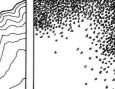

Plotting Shadows in Site Plans

1

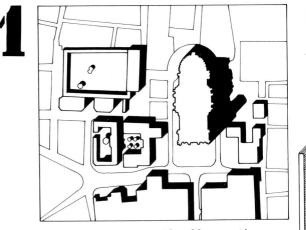

When the degree of detail allows, the projection of shadows provides an invaluable spatial clue to that dimension inherently absent from site plans, i.e., verticality. For instance, shadows emphasize the existence of both the shape of the plan and the height of its implied mass above ground level.

2

Shadows also describe the physical nature of the terrain and, at larger scales and when using open systems of rendering, can hint at its surface texture.

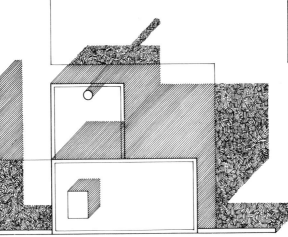

3

Conventionally, shadows in plan are simply a 45-degree projection of the form along an angle of bearing from the bottom left of the drawing. However, shadows can be cast in any convenient projection, i.e., at any angle that does not impede vital information conveyed in the drawing.

4

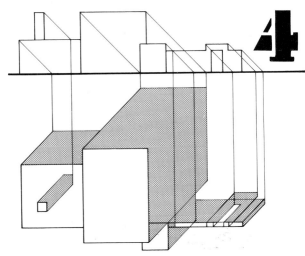

Shadows cast from more complicated forms are plotted with reference to an auxiliary elevation. Therefore, their construction necessitates a degree of familiarity with the building design (see page 56).

Increasingly more complicated forms require the plotting aid of both side and front elevations.

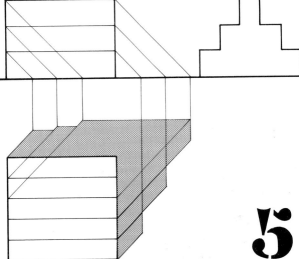

5

6

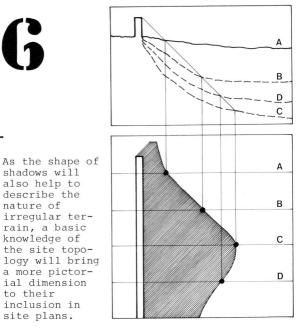

As the shape of shadows will also help to describe the nature of irregular terrain, a basic knowledge of the site topology will bring a more pictorial dimension to their inclusion in site plans.

Plotting Shadows in Floor Plans

1

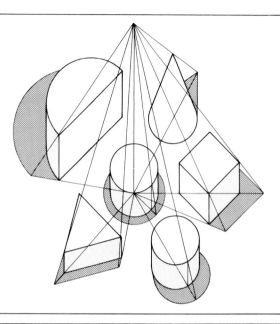

By contrast to the convention that sees the rays of sunlight as parallel and following a single bearing line (see page 22), the rays of light from electric sources are seen as radiating around their point, or points, of source.

Therefore, in plan, electric light rays are plotted to cut all the casting edges of objects, such as furniture, that lie in their path. From this simple principle floor plan shadows can be quickly constructed to represent the effect of overhead lighting patterns.

2

By shading in pencil, ink, wash, or dry-transfer materials, shadows can be invested with different values to simulate strength of light. Also, a value emphasis of any areas of "overlap" will clarify the components of a multishadow cluster.

3

Also, in larger scale interior plans, a multishadowed effect caused by more than one point of source can be represented. Furthermore, light sources of unequal strength or at unequal proximity to the objects in question can be clearly indicated by their corresponding shadows.

4

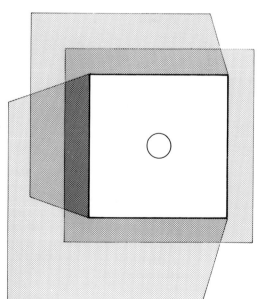

Shadow Projection: Altitude and Azimuth

As the sun arcs across the sky from east to west its overhead position is constantly shifting. Therefore, both the height and the direction of its rays of light are altering continuously--not only by the hour but also by the season.

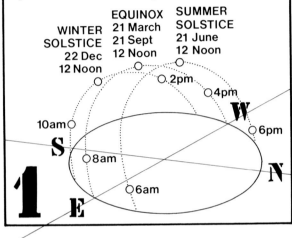

WINTER SOLSTICE 22 Dec 12 Noon

EQUINOX 21 March 21 Sept 12 Noon

SUMMER SOLSTICE 21 June 12 Noon

2pm
4pm
10am
6pm
W
S
8am
N
6am
1
E

2

The effect of altitude is one of two factors used in shadow projection. Altitude refers to the vertical angle formed by the direction of light as it strikes the ground plane. For example, as winter sunlight forms an acute angle with the ground, its shadows are much longer than summer shadows, as are early morning shadows much longer than those at midday.

The geometric convention of shadows cast at an angle of 45 degrees as mentioned on the previous page makes no reference to any aspect or climate. In fact, the actual angle at which the sun strikes the ground in this convention is not 45 degrees but 35 degrees 15 minutes--the altitude for the diagonal of a cube.

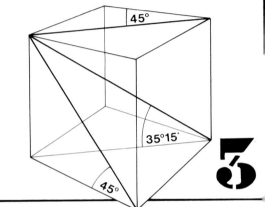

45°
35°15'
45°
3

However, the second feature used in shadow projection is the sun's compass direction in relation to the viewer.

4

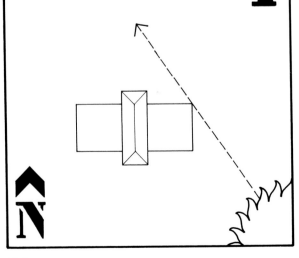

N

This factor refers to the sun's bearing, or azimuth, and is measured in the plan view.

N

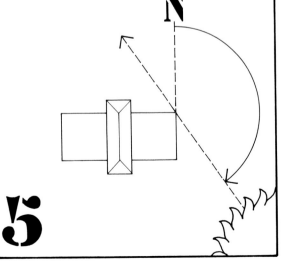

5

BEARING AZIMUTH

N

N

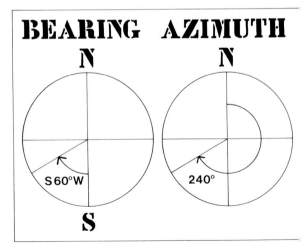

S60°W

240°

S

6

The nonvertical direction of a bearing line is expressed in degrees measured between the directional line and due north or south. Azimuth is measured clockwise from due north and is also expressed in degrees.

A Method of Plotting Shadows in Plan

1

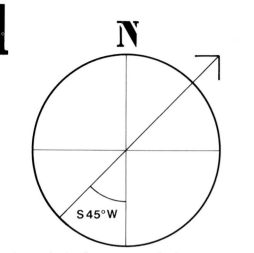

N

S 45° W

basic method of casting shadows accurately
n plans is to first determine the angle of
he sun's bearing for the desired date
nd time, for example, S 45-degrees W (or,
25-degrees azimuth).

2

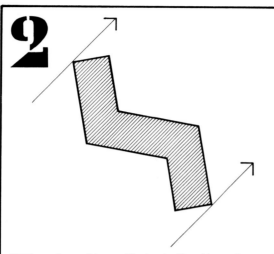

Next, draw lines that strike the edges of
the plan in the direction of this bearing.
This will determine the direction of the
shadow.

3

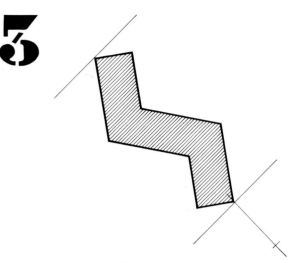

In order to establish the length of the
shadow we must now determine the sun's altitude. To do so, draw a line that is perpendicular to the sun's bearing at a length
equal to the height of the object in plan.

4

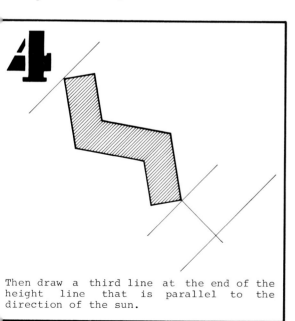

Then draw a third line at the end of the
height line that is parallel to the
direction of the sun.

5

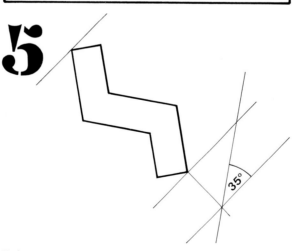

35°

Using a protractor, now construct the chosen
angle of the sun's altitude so that it
bisects the original line describing the
sun's bearing. By the law of similar tri-
angles you will have constructed the altitude
angle on the bearing line at the correct
shadow length.

6

Finally, before rendering the shadow, complete its shape by projecting a line parallel
with the casting edge of the plan. This line
begins at the shadow's length and connects all
other bearing lines.

N.B.: If the top of an object is parallel to
the ground plane it will cast a parallel
shadow.

Two Further Methods of Plotting Shadows in Plan

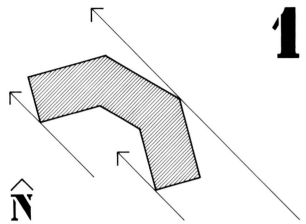

Ñ

This is another method for determining accurate shadows in plan, but this time using an auxiliary elevation.

First strike the corners of the plan with the bearing lines of the sun's rays from the correct direction for the desired time of day and time of year.

1

Then construct an auxiliary elevation of the south facade of the object. This is so we can look at the sun's altitude perpendicularly. Do this by drawing a baseline or ground level parallel to the sun's bearing. Project the edge of the object perpendicular to the new ground line.

N.B.: The object height will remain constant.

2

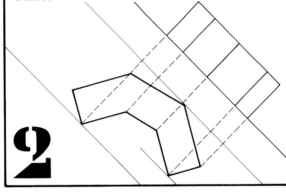

3

Strike the auxiliary elevation with the sun's altitude. For example, we have assumed an altitude of 55 degrees.

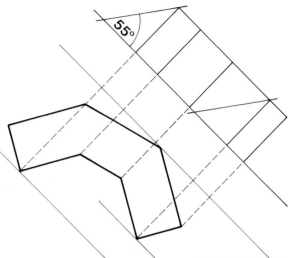

4

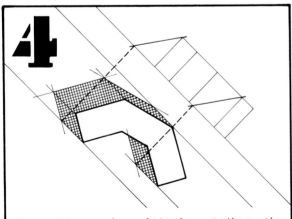

Where the sun's altitude strikes the ground line, project perpendicularly back to the plan until it intersects with the angle of bearing. The length and the direction of the shadow has now been determined. After delineating the shadow's shape, the shadow can be rendered.

5

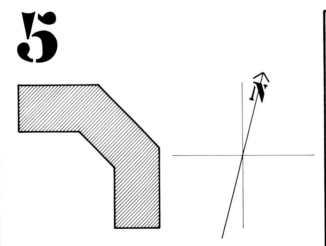

Yet another method of shadow projection in plans begins by drawing a quadrant alongside the building plan so that its axes are parallel with the sides of the plan. A north point is then located on the quadrant.

Next, plot the sun's azimuth on the quadrant; for example, S 45-degrees E. Remember to plot the azimuth from the north-south axis and not from the quadrant axis.

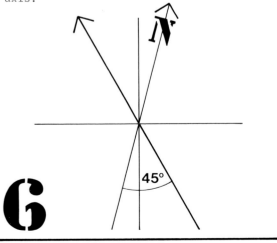

6

Two Further Methods of Plotting Shadows in Plan

Assuming that the vertical quadrant line is a perpendicular pole, and that the horizontal quadrant line is a flat plane seen in elevation, mark off the scaled heights of the building on the vertical pole. Then draw a line at an angle equal to the sun's altitude so that it cuts both the pole at the scaled height and the horizontal quadrant (the sun's altitude is assumed to be 55 degrees).

8

Point A represents a view of the shadow length from the north-south direction. The shadow length from the east-west direction (Point B) is measured on the horizontal axis by striking an arc with a radius equal to that of the length of the shadow.

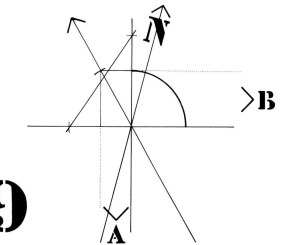

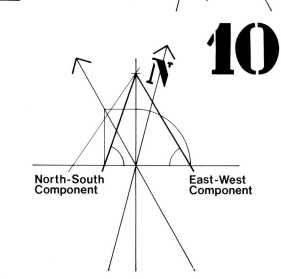

7

55°

Shadow Length

The component of the sun's altitude is determined by transferring the shadow length to the sun's bearing line. The length is then projected onto the horizontal and vertical lines of the quadrant.

9

10

North-South Component

East-West Component

The lines connecting the top of the pole with the shadow length as seen from the quadrant positions form the elevation component for the required position of the sun.

From the points where the elevation component angles intersect with the ground line, project perpendicularly until they intersect with the lines of the sun's bearing on the plan.

11

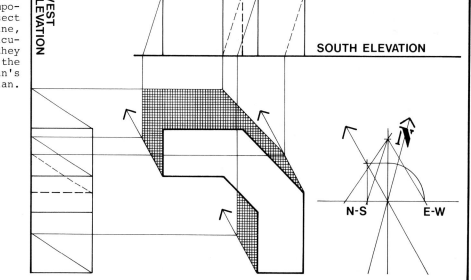

WEST ELEVATION

SOUTH ELEVATION

N-S   E-W

Building Plan as Analytical Diagram

1

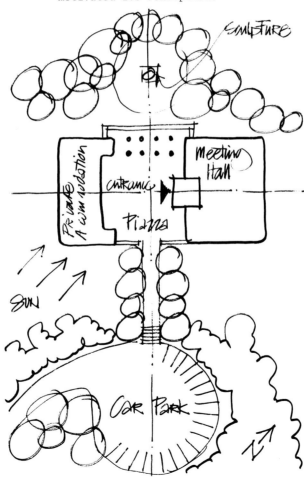

Although we have discussed its pictorial potential, the plan is, in essence, an analytical diagram. In this sense, the plan functions as a graphic mechanism for defining the enclosure of spatial variety. For example, in this plan based on a drawing by the Hardy, Holzman, & Pfeiffer design practice, richly juxtaposed areas of black, white, and gray represent a correspondingly rich spatial arrangement that encourages the viewer to consider the diagram as an abstract organism. In reflecting the structure's inherent organization, the resultant and highly patterned positive-negative design is consistent with the character of its architectural intent. Therefore, when used as an analytical diagram, the plan can be directed to both the investigation and communication of specific aspects of the building design philosophy.

2

For example, a highly useful type of plan is a diagram that, in presentation, acts as an informative link between site analysis findings (see facing page) and the more formal communication of the design solution. Such a diagram is quickly produced to describe the anatomy of an idea and the relationship between the working parts of the building and of the site. Indeed, this diagram simply and clearly conveys the design intent and the main determinants that have motivated its conception.

3

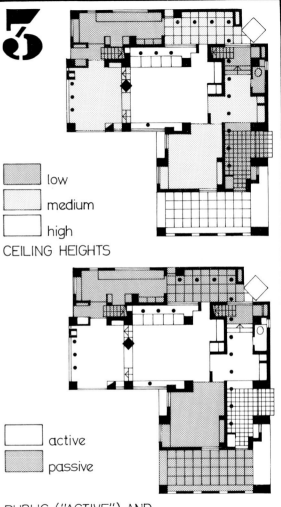

CEILING HEIGHTS

- low
- medium
- high

- active
- passive

PUBLIC ("ACTIVE") AND
PRIVATE ("PASSIVE") INTERACTION

Another use for the analytical plan is in the study and communication of the more subtle or complex relationships of a design. For instance, spatial and functional patterns can be quickly described—the process underlining the formation of a basic interior design philosophy.

Site Plan as Analytical Diagram

1 When applied to contextual analysis, a diagramming process can act as the key informant at the very outset of design. In this diagramming role, the plan provides a vehicle for the on-site collection of physical and non-physical data that, when amalgamated, will shape the development of the decision-making sequence. For instance, a key aspect of environmental design is the effect of light and shade. Therefore the prediction of sun and shadow patterns is an aspect that, when combined with others, will aid the modeling, massing, location, and orientation of an intended built form. Such a study might extend to a more accurate analysis of the sunlight-shadow dynamic along its annual cycle using an auxiliary site model and a Heliodon.

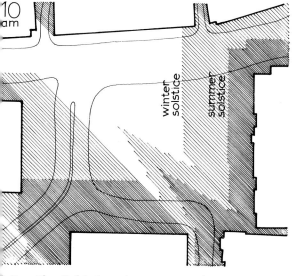

N.B.: The Heliodon is a measuring apparatus comprising a moveable light source and a tilting turntable--its variable coordinates simulating the effects of the sun's movement above a scale site model. Manual 2 describes a method of "printing" the resultant shadow patterns directly on to the model. Otherwise, the information is transferred back to the referent site plan, often enlisting a color code and legend to indicate clearly the individual readings.

Site data basically falls into physical and non-physical categories. For instance, the physical aspects include the age, condition, and materials of existing buildings, together with site topology and attendant drainage and circulation patterns, vegetation and soil type, and so on.

N.B.: It is useful to diagram data directly into the plan as it is collected. If required, plans can later be refined for presentation.

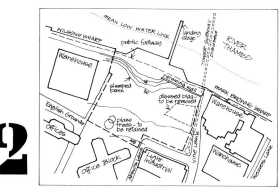

2 The list of ingredients in a site analysis will correspond to the specific nature and complexity of the site. Data for less-complex sites may be confined to a single, composite diagram. Usually produced to a larger scale, the integrated diagram should employ a clear hierarchy of graphic information to avoid confusion.

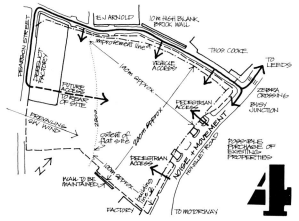

4

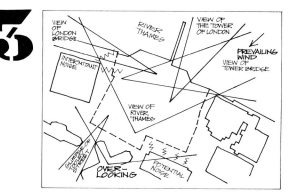

3

The non-physical aspects may involve an analysis of sensory data, such as the location and quality of views both to and from the site, prevailing winds, temperature readings, and the sources of noise or pollutants.

N.B.: The first step is to identify the range of relevant issues required for a thorough analysis.

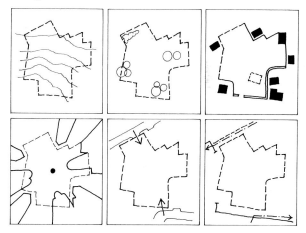

The alternative is to segregate more-complex data into a series of referent diagrams--their number corresponding to the different items included in the analysis. The set may be later presented individually or superimposed in data-related groups using transparent overlays.

5

How to Make "Three-Dimensional" Plans

1

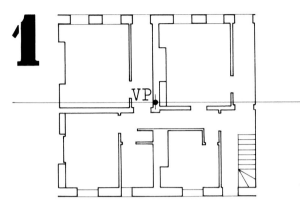

Outside the plan, next locate a second point on the horizon line. We will call this the diagonal point (DP), its distance from the edge of the plan being at least as great as the overall width of the plan.

3

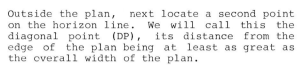
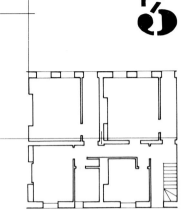

Here is a convenient method of transforming a plan into the "three dimensions" of a more realistic overhead view. After drafting the plan, position a vanishing point (VP) in a central position. This will direct the resultant angle of view.

Then rule a horizontal line through the vanishing point and out to either side of the plan.

Now draw a horizontal measuring line (ML) above or below the area between the plan and the diagonal point. Connect the end of this line to one of the inside faces of the plan wall by means of a vertical line.

2

4

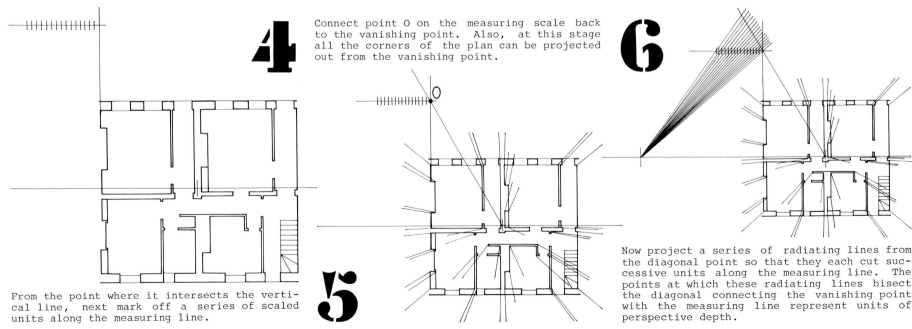

Connect point O on the measuring scale back to the vanishing point. Also, at this stage all the corners of the plan can be projected out from the vanishing point.

6

From the point where it intersects the vertical line, next mark off a series of scaled units along the measuring line.

5

Now project a series of radiating lines from the diagonal point so that they each cut successive units along the measuring line. The points at which these radiating lines bisect the diagonal connecting the vanishing point with the measuring line represent units of perspective depth.

How to Make "Three-Dimensional" Plans

7 This simple perspective plan projection can be used to look upward into a worm's-eye view of interior spaces. As the features shown on the plan will be retained in the front plane of the image, it is simpler to project into the plan rather than outwards as in the overhead view. This is achieved by drawing the measuring line over the plan. Remember to flip the plan over in order to produce the "right-way-round" view from below.

The perspective scale on the diagonal line can now be projected around the walls of the plan to find ceiling level and other scaled heights.

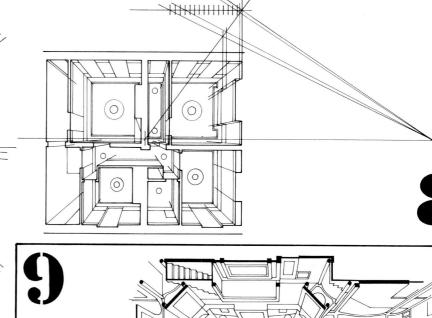

8

Furthermore, the heights of any objects that occur within the space defined by the plan can also be found by transferring the perspective depth scale from a convenient point.

Finally, draw in the details and remove any superfluous construction lines.

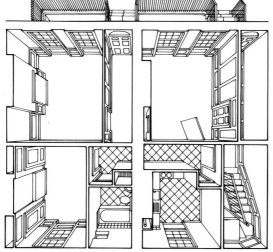

9

The worm's-eye viewpoint is especially useful when showing more complex ceiling plans, such as vaulting. Here is an example based on the work of Robin Evans.

How to Make "Three-Dimensional" Plans

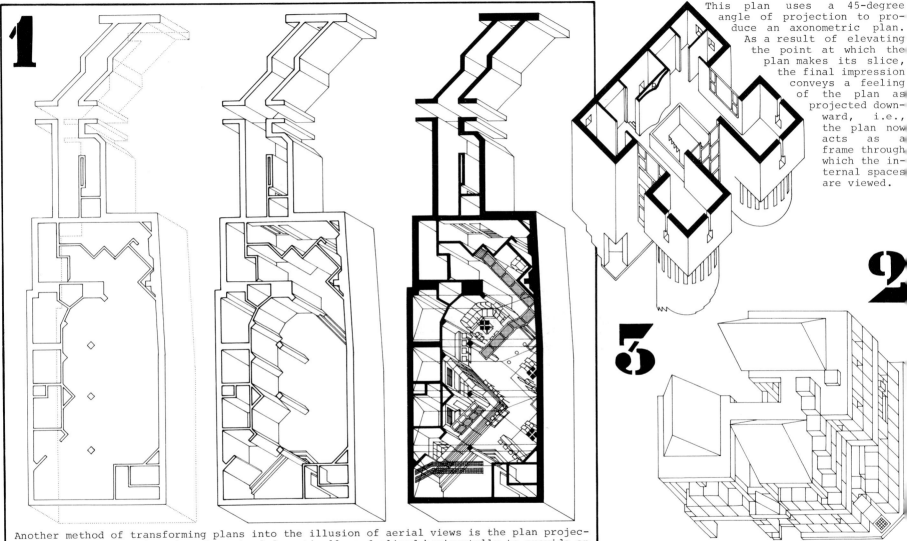

1

2

This plan uses a 45-degree angle of projection to produce an axonometric plan. As a result of elevating the point at which the plan makes its slice, the final impression conveys a feeling of the plan as projected downward, i.e., the plan now acts as a frame through which the internal spaces are viewed.

3

Another method of transforming plans into the illusion of aerial views is the plan projection. To do this the plan is extruded vertically and sliced horizontally to provide an overhead glimpse of interior cells. As each line in the vertical plane is extruded at the same angle, this mode of drawing is simple to construct. It is commonly referred to as a planometric or "shoebox" plan--its potential for bringing a dimension of realism to plans being virtually limitless. Once constructed, surface elaboration may be included on visible wall and floor planes together with appropriately scaled projections of furniture. This drawing is based on the work of Peter Julien.

Using the same simple drafting principles of plan projection, aerial views of a building or of a complex of buildings--complete with their roofs and together with shade and projected shadows--can be quickly constructed. Further variations of plan projection are described on pages 84-95.

2 ELEVATIONS

Introducing the Elevation

1

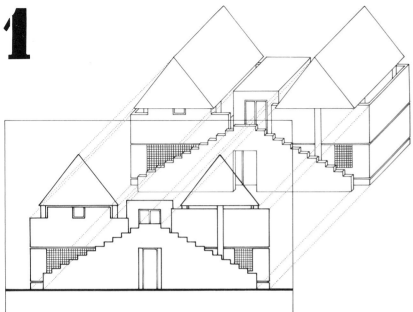

Just as the plan allows the position of any point to be defined in the horizontal plane so, too, it becomes necessary to draw an elevation in order to define a point in the vertical plane. The plan and the elevation must always be read together in order that a three-dimensional concept of a solid be gained from a two-dimensional graphic representation. The elevation joins the plan to bring a head-on view of formal events. To do so, it concertinas all the layers of information in its field of view into a single vertical plane on which--regardless of their position in space --all the forms that are parallel to its line of view retain their true-scale dimensions.

2

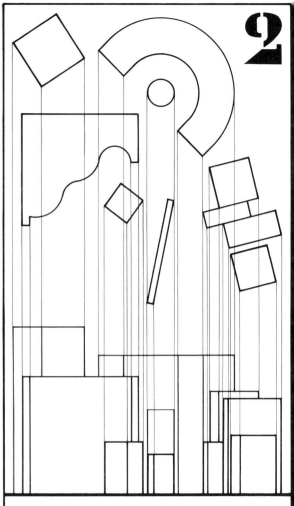

Meanwhile, planes that are not parallel to the elevation's line of view will appear as foreshortened. For example, here are a series of different forms, each with their faces transferred into the apparently spaceless coordinates of the elevation. Notice particularly the way in which the elevation projection deals with curved planes and those not parallel to the drawing surface.

3

However, when dealing with rectangular form the elevation naturally assumes a series of four views that account for the faces, i.e., the front, back, and two sides (or north, south, east, and west) of an object or a building.

When notating elevations, it is important to remember that the points of the compass relate to that facade that addresses them. In other words, a north elevation is seen from the north and a south elevation faces south.

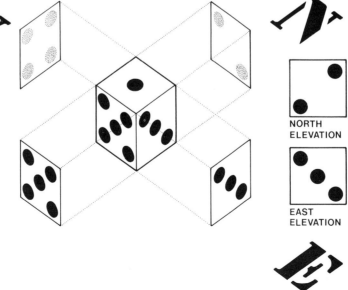

WEST ELEVATION

SOUTH ELEVATION

NORTH ELEVATION

EAST ELEVATION

Introducing the Elevation

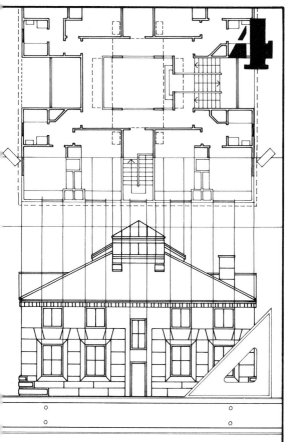

As with all orthographics, it is important to emphasize the difference between a design elevation and a construction elevation. In examining the massing and openings of a facade that may or may not be bathed in light, the design elevation tends to address the client. By contrast the construction elevation communicates the location of elements, materials and their conjunction, and method of construction. When coordinated with other orthographics, this information is addressed to the builder. This drawing is based on the work of the architects, Fielden Clegg.

Elevation drawings of buildings are generally drafted to scales of 1/4" = 1'-0" (1 : 50) or 1/8" = 1'-0" (1 : 100). Like their other orthographic counterparts, they are simple to construct, all planes that are parallel to the drawing surface and perpendicular to the observer's line of vision maintaining their true-scale size, shape, and proportion. As all the parts are drawn equally at the same scale, true measurements can be taken anywhere in the finished drawing. For this reason, they can be projected quickly on transparent drawing material using the plan as an underlay. This drawing is based on a design by Moore, Grover, Harper.

However, we should not forget the interior elevation--used widely by those concerned with interior design. Often termed "wall elevations," these describe the features of internal wall planes and can include objects and events that occur forward of them (see page 48).

Traditionally, architects have concentrated on higher levels of detailing on external rather than internal facades in their building designs. However, the more recent revival of the use of interior "wall elevations" in architectural design signals a return to a more all-embracing design approach. This drawing is based on the work of Michael Graves.

Ambiguity and the Elevation

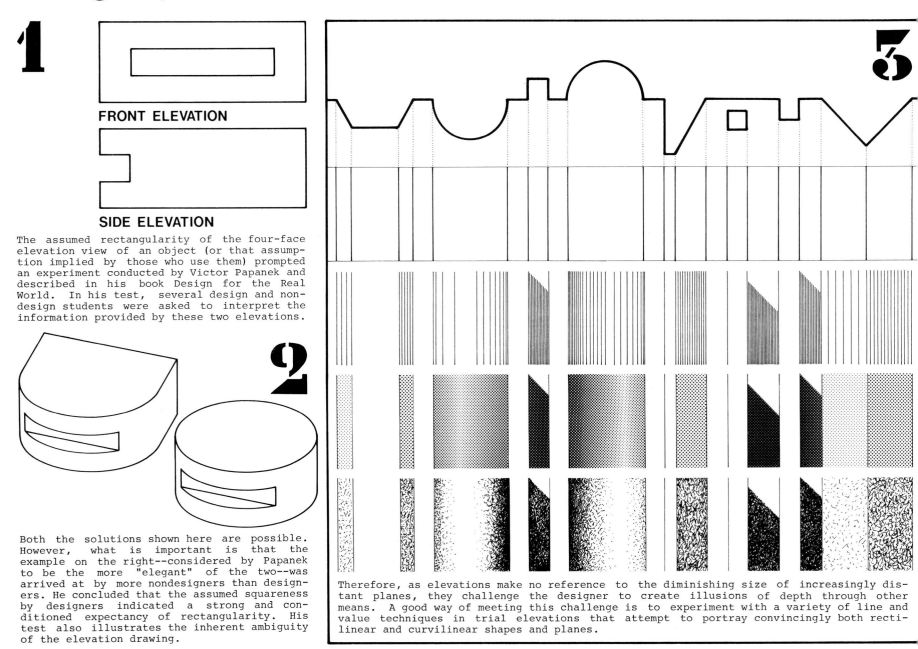

1

FRONT ELEVATION

SIDE ELEVATION

The assumed rectangularity of the four-face elevation view of an object (or that assumption implied by those who use them) prompted an experiment conducted by Victor Papanek and described in his book Design for the Real World. In his test, several design and non-design students were asked to interpret the information provided by these two elevations.

2

Both the solutions shown here are possible. However, what is important is that the example on the right--considered by Papanek to be the more "elegant" of the two--was arrived at by more nondesigners than designers. He concluded that the assumed squareness by designers indicated a strong and conditioned expectancy of rectangularity. His test also illustrates the inherent ambiguity of the elevation drawing.

3

Therefore, as elevations make no reference to the diminishing size of increasingly distant planes, they challenge the designer to create illusions of depth through other means. A good way of meeting this challenge is to experiment with a variety of line and value techniques in trial elevations that attempt to portray convincingly both rectilinear and curvilinear shapes and planes.

Anatomy of an Elevation

A good way of implying a sense of space in presentation elevations is to consider the pictorial opportunities provided by its three basic zones: background, middleground, and foreground.

Background: the sky area and the background landscape or urbanscape may be simply delineated or rendered along a scale of increasingly more detailed information depending on the nature of the setting and the intention of the drawing.

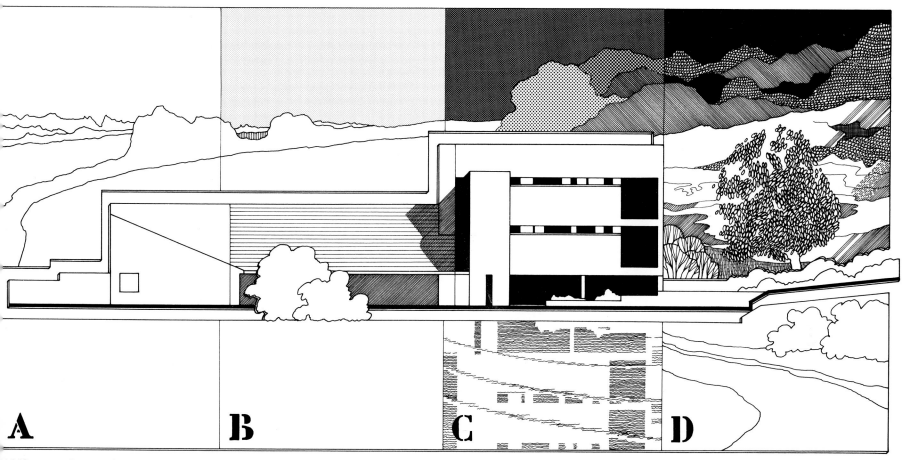

A   B   C   D

Middleground: as this zone occupies the center of implied space in the elevation and also includes the object of the exercise, it acts as the message area. Therefore the middleground usually attracts more detail than elsewhere in the drawing and decisions concerning its degree and technique of application affect the manner in which the other zones are rendered.

Foreground: the amount of implied space, together with the objects it contains, inserted forward of the facade opens up a range of options to the final appearance of the drawing. For example, (A) the elevation can terminate on the baseline, or groundline, immediately in front of the facade; (B) the facade may have objects inserted forward of its plane by conceptually moving the baseline towards the viewer (see page 47); (C) the facade can be reflected into a wet pavement or into adjoining water or (D) have foreground events added that, in recognizing a vanishing point, convert the elevation into the more familiar graphic space of a pseudo-perspective drawing (see page 50).

N.B.: When not elaborating the foreground zone, it is always a good idea to "plant" the facade on a firmly drawn baseline, and to extend the baseline out into adjoining space so that it describes the topographical nature of the immediate setting.

Exploiting the Depth Cues

A means of reducing ambiguity in elevation drawings is to exploit the graphic depth cues that are available to this drawing mode. However, the strongest of all the depth cues, overlap, is inherent in the elevation. The overlap cue is simply that illusion of the third dimension caused when a nearer plane or form partially obscures the view of a more distant plane or form.

This drawing is based on the work of Tim Ronalds.

This particular illusion can be further exploited by emphasizing a dark value immediately behind the silhouettes of planes as they progress back into the "space" of the elevation.

Depth illusion in elevations can also be extended by the introduction of a hierarchy of line weight. This illusion is exploited by using darker, heavier lines to delineate planes nearer the viewer while thinner, lighter lines describe progressively more distant elements.

A further extension of the depth illusion comes with the introduction of atmospheric haze. This cue refers to the darkening of successive planes as they become more distant. An interesting aspect of this visual trick is that its illusion can work in reverse, i.e., darker planes fronting progressively lightening planes. This drawing based on the work of Foster Associates employs both effects.

Exploiting the Depth Cues

6 This sharpness and clarity scale can also be exploited in the detailing of surface finishes. For example, the manipulation of a scale of intensity for the rendering of detail of building materials between front and back planes can stretch the depth illusion. This drawing is developed from an elevation by Nicholas Lacey.

Another graphic expression of atmospheric haze is found in a subtle scale of focus in which frontal planes in elevations possess a sharpness and clarity denied those in the distance. This drawing is based on the work of Rodrigo Perez de Arce.

7 A highly useful graphic device for "modeling" the third dimension in elevations is to flood them with light via the insertion of shade and shadows (see pages 56-59).

N.B.: Shadow rendering allows another opportunity to exploit graphic depth along a scale of atmospheric haze.

Some Basic Rendering Techniques

1 A survey of the more pictorial orthographics of international designers will find the recurrent use of a shading based on the directionality of pencil or pen strokes. This technique is used to imply atmosphere, light, and space on the broader planes of elevations and other orthographics. By restricting the direction of strokes to the diagonal, the technique imparts an underlying sense of order in the rendering together with the potential of generating a wide range of structured value. In order to increase the intensity of value, each series of strokes is layered over the last so that a deepening density of tonal value is built up in an apparently controlled manner throughout the drawing.

2 With some practice this technique can be manipulated not only to develop a personal style but also to provide a wide range of surface textures at various scales that are extremely useful in presentation elevations. For example, this series of details taken from the work of Guiseppe Zambanoni, Romaldo Giurgola, and Cesar Pelli demonstrate respectively how the technique can vary according to personality and the freedom of discipline within which the diagonal stroke is maintained. Furthermore, the work of Pelli shows that when a heavier medium is used, such as wax pencil, the technique is adaptable and capable of a great richness.

Some Basic Rendering Techniques

1 The alternative to the more mechanical appearance of ruled line hatching and cross-hatching is a whole spectrum of freehand hatching that awaits invention by the more adventurous designer. For example, this apparently spontaneous shading technique found in the work of William Henderson extends the diagonal hatching technique into one that involves many directions. Again, this freehand rendering system is, via layering, capable of a rich value scale.

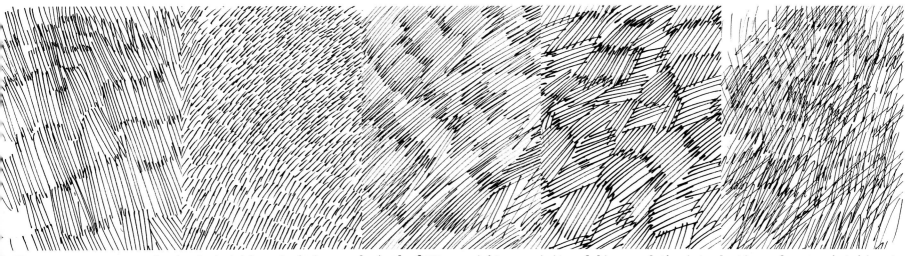

2 Here are some freehand hatching techniques derived from structures of repeated lines or from the repetition of individually drawn clusters of directional lines. Apart from providing ranges of surface quality useful on the facades of buildings, each system relies upon a variation of line weight, proximity of line, and the introduction of cross-hatching to ascend and descend the value scale. These hatching techniques are widely used to bring value to orthographics drafted on transparent drawing materials because they are acceptable for reproduction by the diazo printing process.

41

Rendering Building Materials in Elevations

The selection of scale in elevations is related to the size of the form to be elevated, the function of the drawing and, of course, the size of the drawing paper. However, when drafting elevations at scales of 1/2" = 1' (1 : 20) and upward the opportunity of describing the modular units of building materials is open to the designer. Here are some basic rendering techniques that will prove useful. It is important to note that any variations in the quality of line should respond directly to the constructional appearance of each material (see facing page).

N.B.: Remember that the illusion of depth can be increased by the gradual reduction of line weight intensity or the defocusing of degree of detail on progressively distant planes.

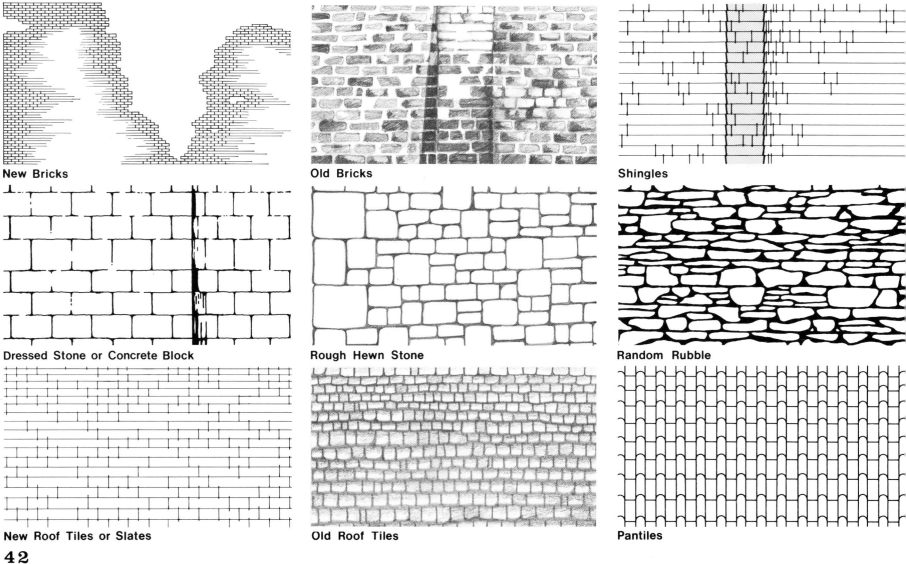

New Bricks

Old Bricks

Shingles

Dressed Stone or Concrete Block

Rough Hewn Stone

Random Rubble

New Roof Tiles or Slates

Old Roof Tiles

Pantiles

Tips When Rendering Building Materials

1 The direct link between an understanding of construction and the appearance of materials in architectural drawings cannot be overstressed. For instance, a common error is to indicate stone facades in a manner that is impossible to construct.

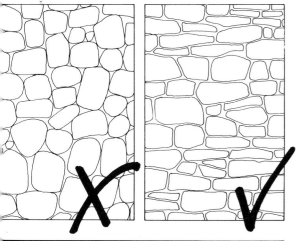

2

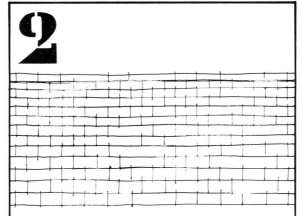

Always sense the method of construction when indicating materials in the illusion of elevations. For example, a slight emphasis on the horizontal lines of rows of roof tiles will suggest a shadow line and a feeling of overlap that occurs at this point.

3 Also, when drawing bricks or blocks avoid bland and toytown effects by allowing the drawing instrument to emphasize junctions between horizontal and vertical mortar joints. Furthermore, a broken line or a considered "hit-and-miss" effect can bring a sensation of light and texture to wall planes.

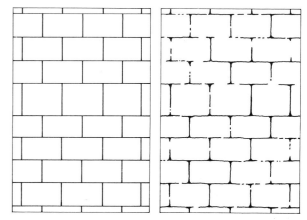

4 Another means of avoiding an over-mechanical appearance of mortar joints is to draw them freehand over lightly penciled and ruled guidelines or, if using transparent drawing material, traced from ruled underlays.

5 Preselected areas of large elevation planes can be rendered to suggest the whole. However, these should not be too isolated. A dramatic lesson is learned in the apocryphal story of one architect who deliberately indicated a few isolated units of masonry on a drawing requiring a builder to repoint a church tower. In misreading the architect's intention, the builder proceeded to stucco the tower exposing only those elements recorded on the drawing.

Rendering Building Materials in Elevations

1

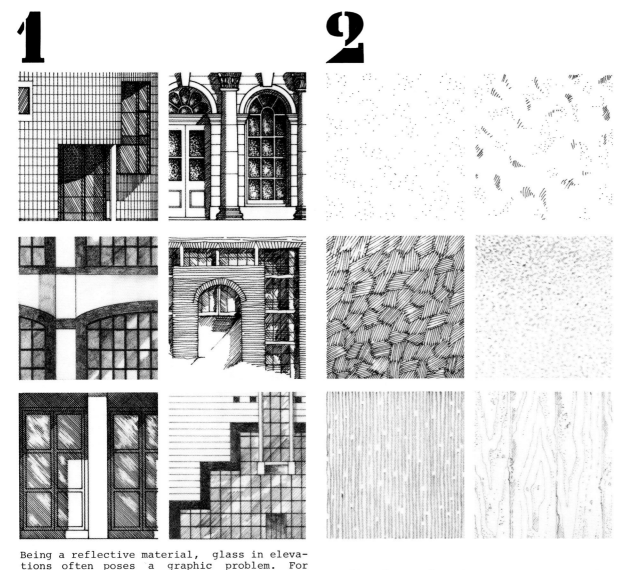

Being a reflective material, glass in elevations often poses a graphic problem. For instance, the widely used dark value ink wash on larger scale drawings tends to depict windows as "eyeless" apertures. However, here are a few techniques for rendering glazing using pencil and pen that recognize the reflective quality of the material.

2

In line-drawn elevations, stucco, concrete, and stone cladding are often indicated with a finely dotted treatment. However, if the scale of the material in the drawing allows, there are several alternative techniques for rendering various surface grains and textures.

3

As any incidental mark within the area of an elevation drawing will register to affect its overall scale, it is important to consider the effect of any surface treatment before insertion. This is particularly relevant when rendering timber in facades--the rendered grain often appearing too gross and shrinking perceptually the impression of the whole. Therefore, it is wise to first delineate the units if timber and then to test a wood grain effect prior to insertion in the drawing.

More Tips When Rendering Building Materials

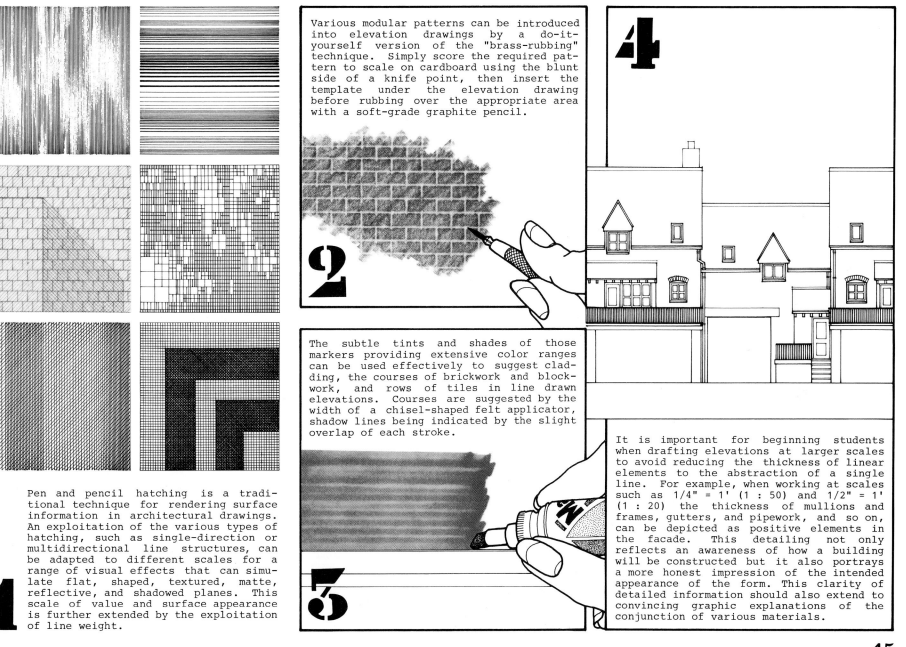

Various modular patterns can be introduced into elevation drawings by a do-it-yourself version of the "brass-rubbing" technique. Simply score the required pattern to scale on cardboard using the blunt side of a knife point, then insert the template under the elevation drawing before rubbing over the appropriate area with a soft-grade graphite pencil.

The subtle tints and shades of those markers providing extensive color ranges can be used effectively to suggest cladding, the courses of brickwork and blockwork, and rows of tiles in line drawn elevations. Courses are suggested by the width of a chisel-shaped felt applicator, shadow lines being indicated by the slight overlap of each stroke.

Pen and pencil hatching is a traditional technique for rendering surface information in architectural drawings. An exploitation of the various types of hatching, such as single-direction or multidirectional line structures, can be adapted to different scales for a range of visual effects that can simulate flat, shaped, textured, matte, reflective, and shadowed planes. This scale of value and surface appearance is further extended by the exploitation of line weight.

It is important for beginning students when drafting elevations at larger scales to avoid reducing the thickness of linear elements to the abstraction of a single line. For example, when working at scales such as 1/4" = 1' (1 : 50) and 1/2" = 1' (1 : 20) the thickness of mullions and frames, gutters, and pipework, and so on, can be depicted as positive elements in the facade. This detailing not only reflects an awareness of how a building will be constructed but it also portrays a more honest impression of the intended appearance of the form. This clarity of detailed information should also extend to convincing graphic explanations of the conjunction of various materials.

Trees: Indicators of Time, Place, and Scale

Because of their climatic variation, together with a wide range of species and stature, and a changing seasonal appearance, trees are great indicators of scale, time, and place. It is a pity therefore that their incidence in elevations is so often ignored or reduced to the anonymity of a pathetic stereotype. With such little effort they can be easily drawn to appear as sympathetic natural elements, both to the technique used in the elevation drawing and to the man-made forms they complement. Here are some ideas for techniques that are derived from observation. They are arranged in varying scale together with the attendant opportunity for detail.

N.B.: If designing for an existing site where trees will play an important role in the resulting act of architecture, it is a good idea to sketch specimens directly on site, or to photograph them for later reference.

46

See-Through Trees for Elevations

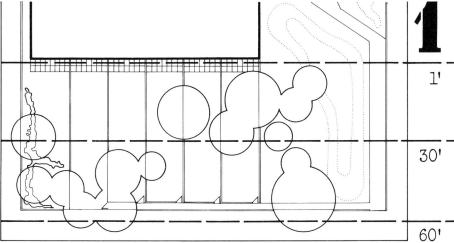

1

1'

30'

60'

Decisions concerning the inclusion or exclusion of landscape elements situated forward of the facade seen in elevation drawings stem from the degree of contextual information required for the drawing. This decision represents the determination of the point at which the section is cut across the line of vision.

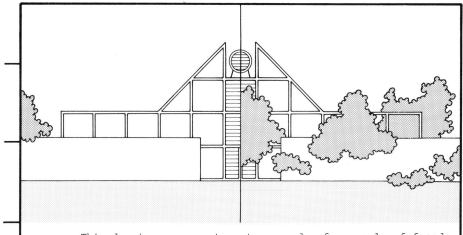

2 This drawing represents extreme ends of a scale of facade exposure. At one end of the scale is the common method of total facade exposure while restricting contextual information to either side. At the other is a viewing stance that, in accounting for elements that lie in the field of vision, allows glimpses of the built form.

 3 One method of including trees forward of a facade while still clearly exposing fenestration detail is to place the design in a winter setting.

However, an effective compromise is to allow a penetrating view through foliage such as in this elevation based on a drawing by the Fielden-Clegg Partnership. Here, a **4** fine-line outlines tree forms and suggests foliage while the integrity of the hatched facade is maintained by recording only its main outlines within the "hidden" areas of the facade.

Interior Wall Elevations

Interior elevations result from the desire to depict the features and fixtures of one or more significant internal wall planes from the four axial views provided by a cubic space. As the wall is "removed" from the designed space in order to isolate it for the drawing, the line defining the outer edge of an interior elevation, i.e., the boundary shape of the vertical plane, will, automatically, be a section line. However, when this section line is given substance, i.e., when the building fabric is cut through to expose graphically the construction details of materials within the thicknesses of walls, floors, and ceilings, the drawing becomes a hybrid graphic known as a sectional elevation (see page 67).

These are portions of two presentation wall elevations showing a discotheque bar designed by Peter Julien and drawn at two different scales. The one on the left is the more traditional wall elevation describing events forward of the main wall, such as chairs, luminaires, bar, and raised and lowered horizontal planes, all at the same scale. Meanwhile, the elevation on the right, although conforming to the same-scale treatment of overlapping planes inherent in this orthographic view, begins to exploit the illusion of perspective in its details. For instance, notice the hint of shadow on the stairs, and that the figures and spotlights appear as they would in perspective. Furthermore, the size difference between "near" and "far" spotlights adds the kind of comparative size distortion that we associate with depth.

These drawings are based on the work of Peter Julien.

Transfer Technique for Wall Elevations

1

Apart from using magazine photographs as the source of tracings and drawings, or as collage for the insertion of figures, trees, automobiles, and other entourage in elevations, is a method that involves the direct transfer of their color inked images using solvents. When used carefully this technique can bring an element of conviction to the details of an elevation, the transferred image often blending successfully with the overall quality of the orthographic. First introduced briefly in Manual of Graphic Techniques 1, the technique relies upon a solvent, such as white spirit, nail polish remover (acetone), methylated spirits, silk screen cleaning fluid, or printer's ink solvent. The most efficient solvent for the type of magazine photograph used will be found by experiment, but it is recommended that transfer tests begin by using color magazines printed on the less glossy papers.

2

After selecting an appropriate color magazine photograph that is in scale with that of the elevation, it should be cut out leaving a generous margin around the required image. Then place it face down on clean paper and coat liberally with the solvent.

3

Next position the photograph face down on the elevation drawing before working over the back of the area to be transferred.

N.B.: The application of solvent will both loosen the ink and allow the image to be seen from the back of the paper during transfer.

4

Finally, gently peel away the exhausted magazine paper to reveal the transferred image. If the pressure-transfer has been successful, an apparently drawn but "printed" image is integrated into the artwork.

This elevation detail includes transfer figures produced by Adrian Griffiths, a fifth-year architecture student at Oxford Polytechnic. The figures were transferred using white spirit as the solvent. Transfer figures from color magazines work well in line drawings and can also be successfully integrated into colored pencil drawings--especially when the same directional stroke is used for both the transfer and color rendering technique.

Elevations as Pseudo-Perspectives

1 The traditional exterior elevation is a hybrid graphic because its groundline, or baseline, usually functions as a vertical sectional cut through the land mass and any incidental forms immediately forward and across the face of the building.

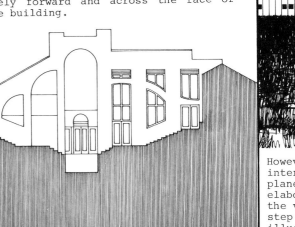

2

However, this frontal zone is sometimes interpreted graphically as a horizontal plane rather than a vertical slice. Its elaboration as a surface occurring between the viewer and the facade marks the first step away from abstraction and toward the illusion of space.

3 Once the decision to convert the elevation has been made, the introduction of single-point perspective coordinates using the vanishing point to target a key element in the facade will transform the elevation into a powerful illusion of space.

4

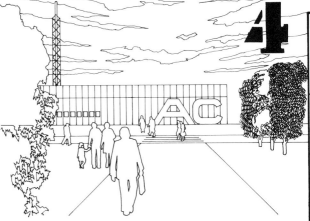

Generally speaking, the insertion of objects and figures that are harnessed by single-point convergence should support and frame rather than impede the view of the facade.

N.B.: The insertion of cloud formations that also respond to the diminishing effect of apparent size is a further development of the pseudo-perspective.

5

The treatment of this zone as a perspective is often stretched to include large areas of foreground space, particularly when the need to portray a building with associated activities is paramount.

Elevations as Pseudo-Perspectives

1

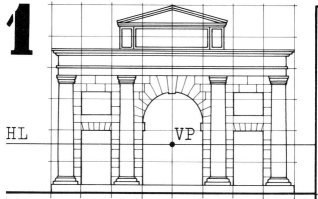

HL   VP

To convert an exterior or interior elevation into a pseudo-perspective, first superimpose a lightly drawn grid over the facade. Then insert a horizon line (HL) at a scaled eye level height above the groundline. A vanishing point (VP) that will concentrate the resultant angle of view on an important feature should now be spotted on a point on the horizon line, such as a main entrance.

2

Next, project lines from the vanishing point that radiate out towards the viewer, making sure that they each intersect the points at which the vertical grid lines superimposed on the elevation touch the groundline.

3

By extending the units of measurement represented by the vertical grid lines on the groundline out to either side of the elevation, the entire width of the foreground plane can be filled with lines of convergence.

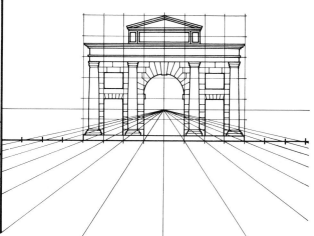

4

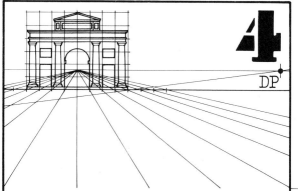

DP

Now locate a diagonal point (DP) on the horizon line out to the extreme right or left of the elevation. The distance of this point from the vanishing point should be at least one and a half times the width of the elevation. Strike a line from the diagonal point to that it bisects the nearest, lower corner of the facade on the groundline.

5

The points at which this diagonal line intersects the foreground radiating lines fixes scaled units of depth that increase as they approach the viewer. These can be extended horizontally to complete the measured plane of the foreground perspective grid.

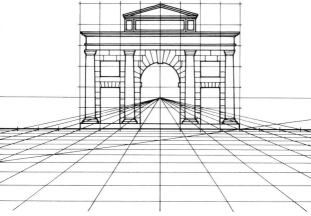

6

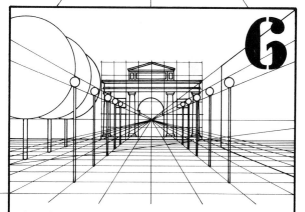

The foreground grid will now guide the accurate location and delineation of objects that occupy the illusion of space between viewer and facade. Heights in this perspective are easily found by projecting lines out from the vanishing point and through the appropriate scaled point on the original facade grid.

51

Sky Mass as Positive Element

Traditionally, the area of sky above facades drawn in elevations is left blank in order not to detract from the information represented in the building. However, apart from the implied sky hinted at by some shading either immediately behind the skyline (to contrast with light-colored forms) or along the upper frame (to suggest an "overhead" feeling), the inclusion of an appropriately rendered sky area can bring a sense of drama to elevated facades. These can range from the suggestion of atmospheric haze to a variety of skies filled with cloud formations--some using their diminishing size to convey depth (see page 38). Here are six freehand and mechanically drafted sky techniques, three using line and three using value. Like all other contextual detail used in orthographics, their selected treatment should be conducive both to the scale adopted and to the technique employed elsewhere in the drawing.

Reflections in Elevations

1

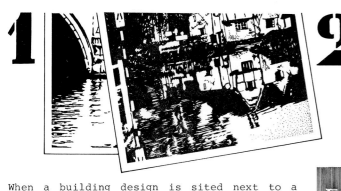

When a building design is sited next to a pool, river, lake, or sea, always take advantage of using the surface of water as a reflecting plane in which appears an inverted image of what is shown above the waterline. However, as water is in a constant state of movement it is difficult to study. Therefore it is a good policy to collect a series of photographs illustrating water reflections in various states of agitation. These can then be adapted to various techniques in mirrored elevations.

Yet another technique begins with a series of vertical guidelines that respond to the width of formal events in the elevation. These lines then guide the insertion of clusters of freehand horizontal lines whose location and weight reflect invertedly the areas of value in the overhead facade.

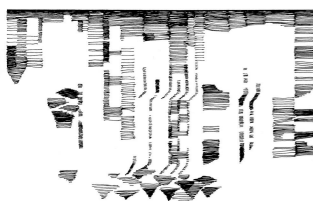

2

For example, one schematic technique for rendering reflections is achieved by either ruling or freehand drawing a sequence of vertical lines that respond to reflecting lines above the waterline. Also, the vertical lines can, using a "hit-and-miss" technique, be broken intermittently to suggest the effect of light catching the water's surface. On tracing paper this effect can be produced by using a razor blade or ink eraser to "lift" parts of the lines.

4

Working directly from photographs can also inform a three-value system of wave-like shapes that is easily rendered to respond mirror-fashion to the juxtaposition of value in events above the waterline.

N.B.: The value system in reflections usually appears darker than its counterpart in the reflecting image.

3

Another variation of this effect for painted elevations is a dry-brush technique. The simulated reflection is caused by dragging a lightly loaded hog brush downward from the edge of the reflecting plane to a length that responds to the height of forms occurring above it.

A more frivolous but effective version of this technique is the application of clusters of line-flecks that can simulate various degrees of surface disturbance. This technique is the quickest of those described here and can be most convincing.

6

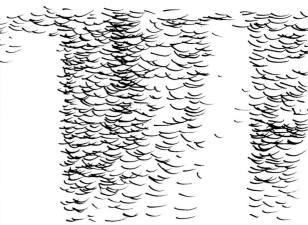

A Technique for After-Dark Elevations

1

The appearance of a building will be transformed completely as it moves from its traditionally rendered daytime experience to that of a nighttime impression. As the source of illumination switches from sunlight to the more localized electric sources occurring immediately outside, on, or inside the building, mass dissolves and surfaces glow, the viewer being drawn to light patterns and given the opportunity of catching glimpses into interiors. Therefore the scope of the nocturnal setting might be considered for elevations, especially when the design exercises a positive after-dark function, or when the fenestration suggests such exploitation. Here is an economical and effective technique for showing nighttime elevations illustrated in a drawing produced in the early 1930s showing neon lighting on a movie theater. It is drawn at a scale of 1/8" = 1' (1 : 100) and the mediums used are white and black crayon together with red and yellow poster paint and pastels on black paper.

2

3 Next take an orange-red pastel and an old container lid. Gently scrape the side of the pastel with a knife blade until you have a small deposit of powder in the lid.

4 To simulate the aura of the neon strips, double over the corner of a soft cloth, such as a duster, and wrap it around the end of a paintbrush handle. Dip the end into the powder and rub it along the line of the neon tube to give a concentrated effect along its run and around the ends of the "glowing" bands. Blow away any surplus, and with a clean finger lightly rub the edges to achieve a consistent fading effect.

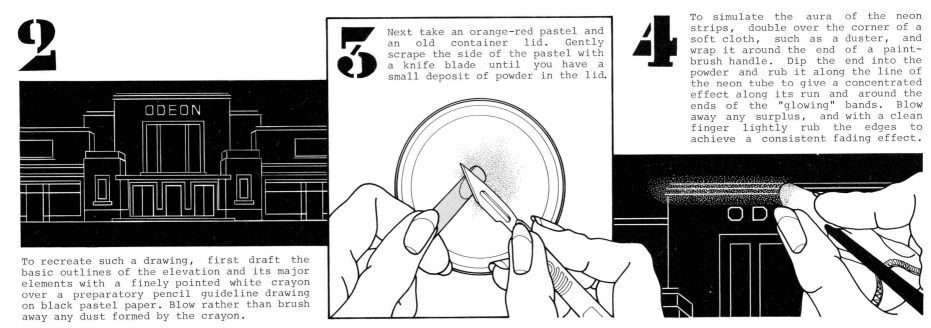

To recreate such a drawing, first draft the basic outlines of the elevation and its major elements with a finely pointed white crayon over a preparatory pencil guideline drawing on black pastel paper. Blow rather than brush away any dust formed by the crayon.

A Technique for After-Dark Elevations

5

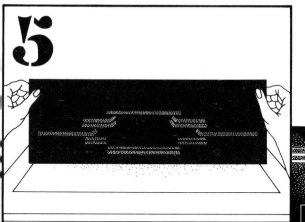

If any surplus powder remains on the drawing after blowing, do not attempt to brush it off as this will cause streaking. Instead, lift the drawing off the board and tap its edge onto the board to remove any residue.

Next take a lime-yellow pastel to insert the scattered light effect of fluorescent lamps under the central canopy and behind first floor glazing. Prepare some yellow powder, invert the drawing on the board and mask the top of the drawing with a thin card. Gently finger-rub the powder along this line and blend the edges. The color mixture of the yellow pastel with the black paper will give a greenish tinge that simulates effectively the color of fluorescent lamps.

8

6

To complete the neon tubes first dilute some orange-red poster paint with a little water--sufficient to enable it to flow easily in a ruling pen, but not enough to destroy its opacity. Rule a thick line along the position of the neon tube, using a ruler with tapered edges so that the paint will not bleed beneath it. Allow to dry fully.

9

The pastel rendering stage is completed by the indication of reflected light of both neon and fluorescent lights on the sidewalk. This is achieved by mixing the remains of the red and yellow pastel dust and finger-rubbing along the mask placed above the groundline. The resultant orange mix is faded-off as it descends into the pavement zone.

7

Then mix some yellow paint and adjust the ruling pen to give a finer line. Rule lightly over the center of the red line. Do not press too hard as the layer of red paint may flake.

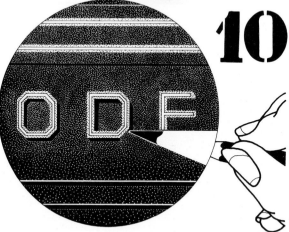

10

Finally add emphasis to the drawing by ruling in shadow lines with a soft black crayon under ledges and window frames. Spray very lightly with a suitable fixative. Allow to dry and apply another coat of fixative. Do not oversaturate the image with fixative as this will loosen the pastel.

Plotting Shadows in Elevations

As with the projection of shadows in plan, shadows cast across the face of elevations follow a convention that assumes the sun to be in a fixed position, i.e., emanating parallel rays of light from top left along a bearing angle of 45 degrees.

ELEVATION

To plot the shadow of a square column standing forward of an elevation plane, reference is made to an auxiliary plan. First project 45-degree lines from the corners of its elevation together with similar projections from the plan.

PLAN

1

2 Where the lines projected on plan make contact with the vertical plane (in plan), perpendicular lines are projected upward to intersect the 45 degree projections on the elevation.

3 The resulting intersections will find the outline of the shadow in elevation. Once plotted they are ready for rendering.

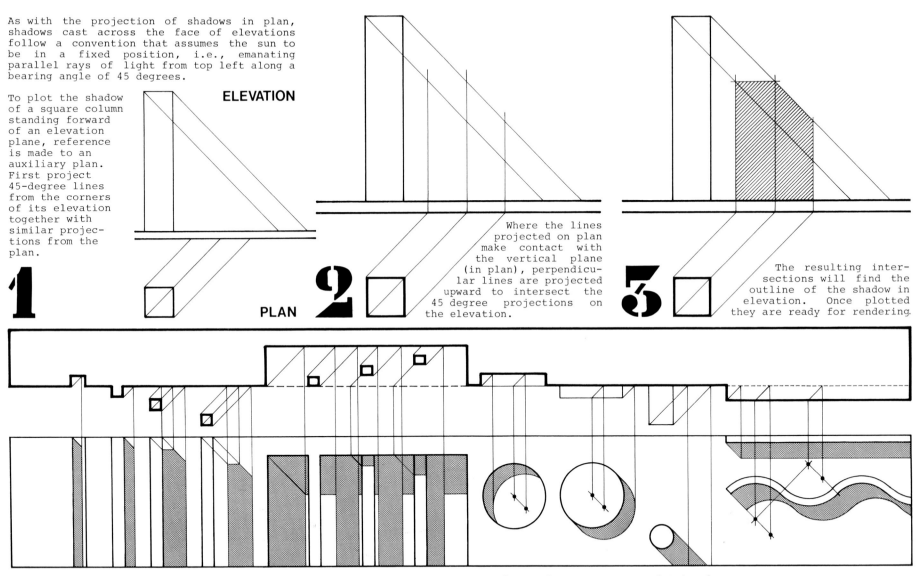

4 Using this basic setup, a whole range of shadows that result from recesses, projections, and objects forward of the elevation can be quickly plotted. The effect of the 45-degree shadow convention appears convincing as it corresponds to average daylight conditions. Also, as the dimensions of shadows are generally the same as the objects from which they are cast, construction is fast using a T-square and triangle.

N.B.: Notice that the shadows cast from the cylinder and cylindrical recess are found by slipping the circle along the appropriate direction of the 45-degree angle to a length equal to their depth.

Plotting Shadows on Inclined Planes

1 The plotting method for shadows cast from a chimney onto a pitched roof follows the principles already established. An auxiliary section or side elevation is necessary in order to find the point at which the shadow from the top of the stack strikes the inclined plane.

3 The equivalent points A, B, C, and D on the front elevation are now projected along the 45-degree bearing of the shape of the shadow on the pitched roof. Notice that only when a shadow is cast from one parallel plane to another is the edge of the shadow at the same angle as the casting edge.

2 To plot the shadow from a dormer window, first project points A, B, C, and D on an auxillary side elevation back at 45 degrees onto the inclined plane. The points of intersection are then transferred horizontally to the front elevation.

4 This architectural form together with its shadow projection is one of the most recurrent in building design presentation.

5 To plot the shadow of the form forward of the main elevation, first project points A, B, and C along the 45-degree bearing of the sun on an auxiliary side elevation. If the line projected from A intersects the roof, extend the line of the slope to cut the line projected from B. This will establish the secondary angle of the shadow on the roof plane. Next transfer all points of intersection horizontally to the front elevation.

6 Now, from the equivalent points A, B, and C on the front elevation, project the 45-degree shadow casting lines. Their intersection with the appropriate horizontal projection will form the shape of the shadow cast on roof and wall planes.

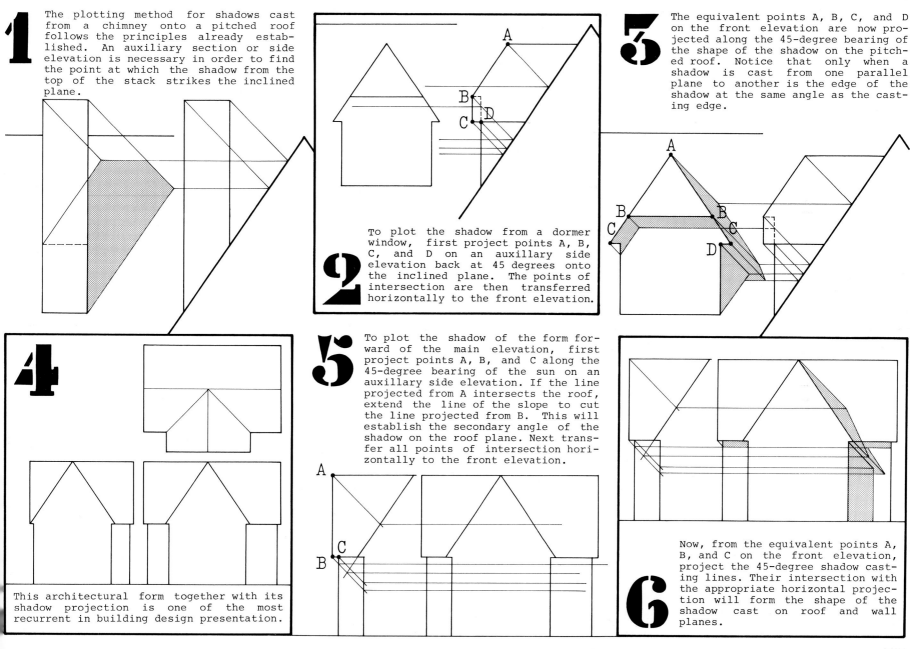

Plotting Shadows from Circular Planes

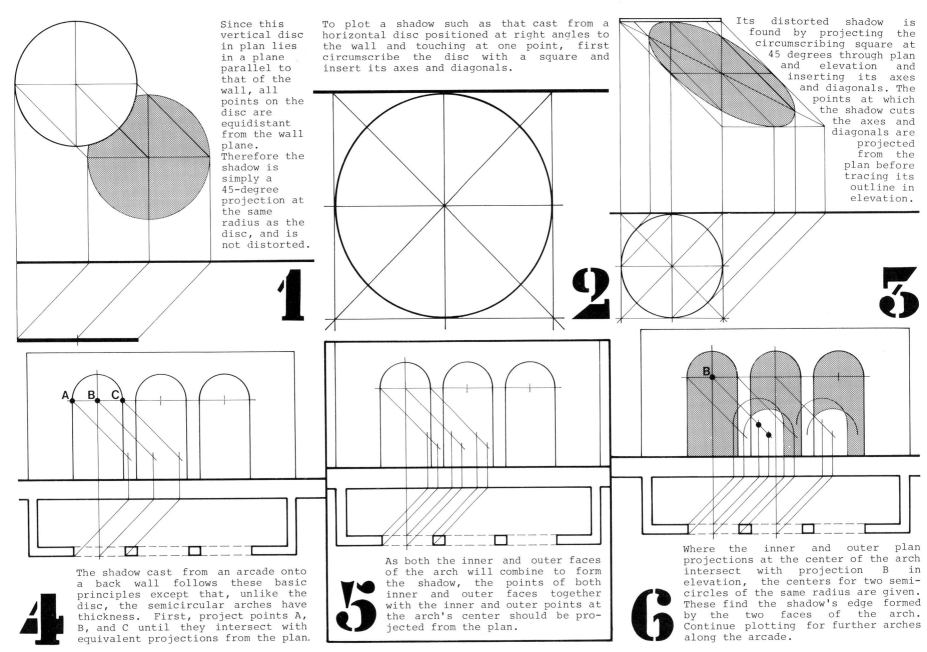

Since this vertical disc in plan lies in a plane parallel to that of the wall, all points on the disc are equidistant from the wall plane. Therefore the shadow is simply a 45-degree projection at the same radius as the disc, and is not distorted.

1

To plot a shadow such as that cast from a horizontal disc positioned at right angles to the wall and touching at one point, first circumscribe the disc with a square and insert its axes and diagonals.

2

Its distorted shadow is found by projecting the circumscribing square at 45 degrees through plan and elevation and inserting its axes and diagonals. The points at which the shadow cuts the axes and diagonals are projected from the plan before tracing its outline in elevation.

3

The shadow cast from an arcade onto a back wall follows these basic principles except that, unlike the disc, the semicircular arches have thickness. First, project points A, B, and C until they intersect with equivalent projections from the plan.

4

As both the inner and outer faces of the arch will combine to form the shadow, the points of both inner and outer faces together with the inner and outer points at the arch's center should be projected from the plan.

5

Where the inner and outer plan projections at the center of the arch intersect with projection B in elevation, the centers for two semicircles of the same radius are given. These find the shadow's edge formed by the two faces of the arch. Continue plotting for further arches along the arcade.

6

58

Plotting Shade on Spherical Planes

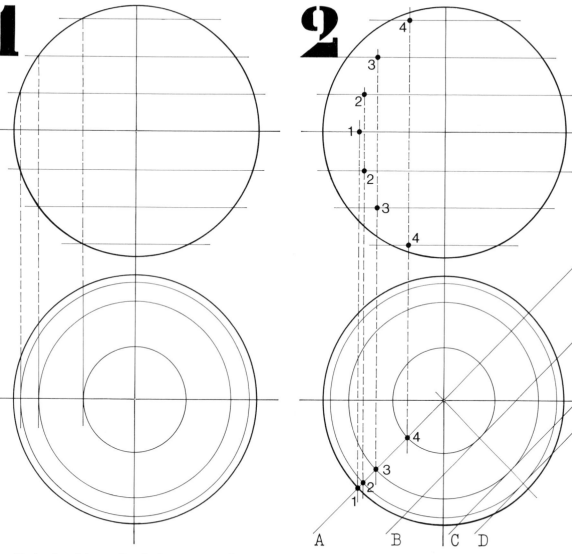

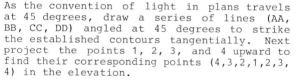

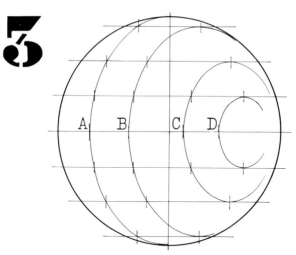

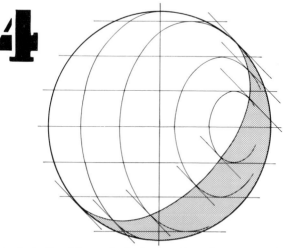

Having plotted and established the resulting contour with a continuous line, repeat the transfer process by projecting up the equivalent points along the remaining section lines BB, CC, DD, on plan to find their corresponding contours on the elevation.

To find the line of shade on a sphere in elevation, first draw a series of equally spaced horizontal lines above and below its diameter. Then project down their points of intersection with its circumference to find their equivalent contours along the diameter in plan.

As the convention of light in plans travels at 45 degrees, draw a series of lines (AA, BB, CC, DD) angled at 45 degrees to strike the established contours tangentially. Next project the points 1, 2, 3, and 4 upward to find their corresponding points (4,3,2,1,2,3, 4) in the elevation.

To plot the line of shade on the elevation of the sphere, finally strike tangential lines at 45 degrees that represent the parallel rays of light to touch each of the contours. A continuous line drawn through these points will establish the line of shade in elevation.

How to Make "Three-Dimensional" Elevations

1

This technique involves the construction of a relief image from an elevation drawing of a building via a layering process using a series of card-mounted diazo prints. The original drawing should be executed on tracing paper or other transparent drawing material. The technique works well when the original is a line drawing that exploits line weights and is also enhanced when shadows are cast from projecting elements in the design. It is also good for communicating street elevations, especially those including groups of buildings, trees, people, automobiles, and so on.

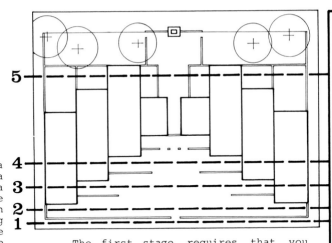

2

The first stage requires that you establish the number of diazo prints required to assemble the relief. To do this, refer to the site plan and count the number of changes in plane along the direction of view represented by the elevation drawing.

3

Proceed to print the appropriate number of identical diazo prints on good quality white print paper. These should then each be heat mounted or aerosol adhesive spray mounted onto cardboard backing sheets.

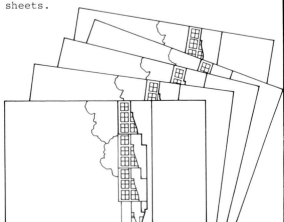

4

Next, take one of the mounted diazo prints. This will act as the background sheet or "baseboard" on which the ensuing stages of lamination will be assembled.

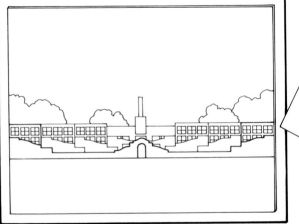

5

Now take a second mounted diazo print and, using a sharp Stanley knife, proceed to carefully cut away the sky area by a precision cut along the sky-line.

6

This cutaway portion of the elevation should now be aerosol adhesive spray mounted directly over its counterpart on the "baseboard" diazo print.

N.B.: At this stage and between each ensuing lamination it may be necessary to place a weighted board over the newly glued layer in order to ensure a good bond.

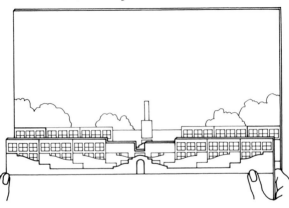

How to Make "Three-Dimensional" Elevations

7 Now take a third card-mounted diazo print and again cut along the skyline in order to remove the sky mass. However, this time all other portions of the elevation that occupy a background plane already represented in the previously laminated diazo print should also be carefully removed.

When the cutting stage is completed, glue this laminate into position on the relief.

N.B.: The three-dimensional quality of the relief relies upon the progressive cutting away of background elements as the assembly is built up. The gradual buildup of laminates leaves behind fragments of the elevation that exist at their predetermined plane in the relief--thereby giving a strong sense of depth. Meanwhile, planes that will appear in the final laminate remain intact throughout the entire assembly.

8

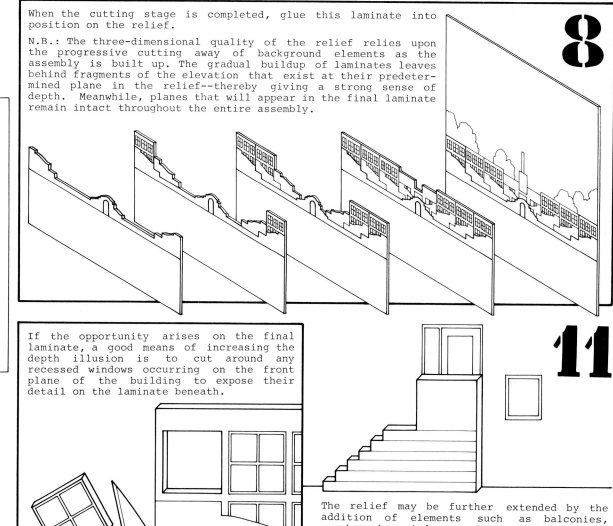

If the opportunity arises on the final laminate, a good means of increasing the depth illusion is to cut around any recessed windows occurring on the front plane of the building to expose their detail on the laminate beneath.

11

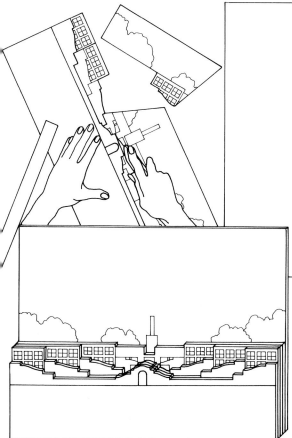

Continue this selective cutting and gluing sequence with the remaining card-mounted diazo prints until the final laminate (the plane nearest the viewer) is established on the relief.

9 **10**

The relief may be further extended by the addition of elements such as balconies, porches, bay windows, and so on, that would occur forward of the building plane. To save printing an extra diazo print for this purpose, such elements can--with preplanning--be removed from a lower level in the relief and set aside for later use.

N.B.: The holes left by the removal of these elements will be concealed by subsequent layers of diazo print.

61

How to Make "Stageset" Elevations

1 Here is another technique for making elevations appear as three-dimensional presentations. At its simplest the technique works well using elevations with a horizontal bias, such as those of long, low buildings, street elevations, and the like. The depth effect is achieved when the foreground section appears as a cutout and positioned approximately 1/4" (6mm) forward of the main drawing.

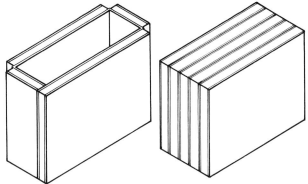

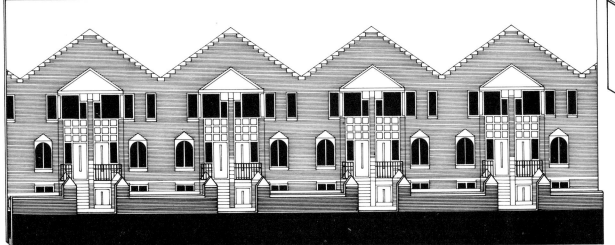

2 This "stageset" approach to presentation elevations can be produced from two or more card-mounted prints of the same drawing, or from an original drawing worked specifically for this purpose on two or more sheets of paper. The cutout components of the "stageset" elevation are then glue assembled using spacer pads made from either folded paper or laminated blocks of card.

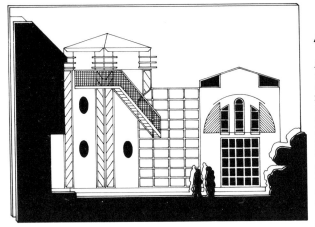

3 Provided the technique responds to the spatial demands of the elevation, it can be applied in a variety of ways. For instance, another two-layered version might detach foreground buildings to produce a framed view.

4 A version employing three layers might separate foreground from middleground (the latter containing the building design) with a third layer acting as backdrop and carrying sky and background information.

N.B.: Notice that the technique can be worked successfully with drawings exclusively in line. However, the depth illusion can be further extended by the addition of color or a progressively darkening or lightening value sequence between foreground and background planes.

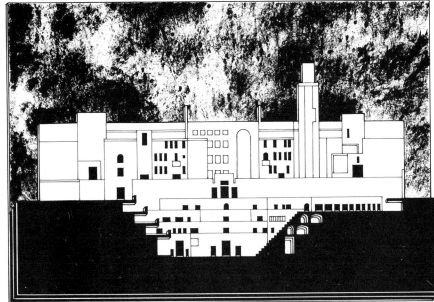

3 SECTIONS

Introducing the Section

1 The section drawing represents a perpendicular true-to-scale cut made through the solid and void of a three-dimensional idea. In other words, it usually functions as an upright plan view resulting from the conceptual removal of a portion of the form under study so that a pre-selected head-on view of its internal cells and partitions is revealed.

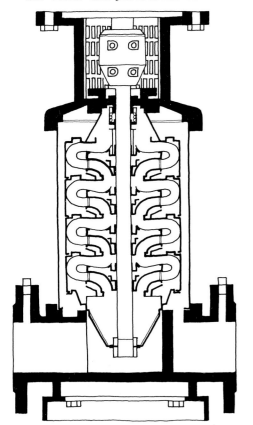

In so doing, the section joins the orthographic views offered by the plan and the elevation to complete the set of single-view diagrams that collectively convey a totally dimensioned and three-dimensional record of an object or a building.

2

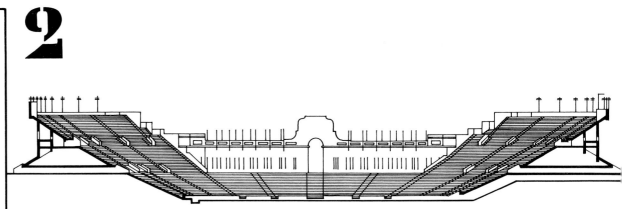

If the plan is seen as the generator of design thinking, then the section acts as a critical witness to its three-dimensional understanding during the evolution of a design. Commonly drawn to scales of 1/8" = 1' (1 : 100) or 1/4" = 1' (1 : 50), the section is considered by many architects to be the most important and incisive design tool in architectural graphics. This is because the result of its graphic surgery takes us towards the very essence of the anatomy of our formal ideas. Therefore, the main consideration in its cutaway operation is the location of the incision. In design sections this should be fixed upon a line from which the greatest number of internal spatial relationships can be visualized.

3

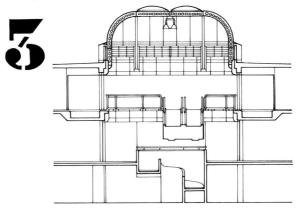

To avoid confusion in design sections, the slice is usually made along one continuous plane. However, it is important to locate the line of the section so that it cuts through key architectural points, such as major changes in level and openings in the structure. In other words, avoid slicing through secondary elements, such as ducts and columns, as these may be misread as major partitions in the section.

There are two basic directional cuts. One is represented by the cross-section that bisects a form laterally.

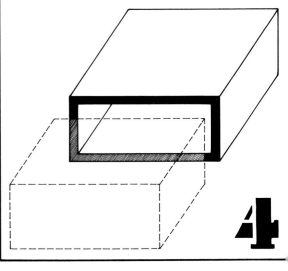

4

Introducing the Section

5

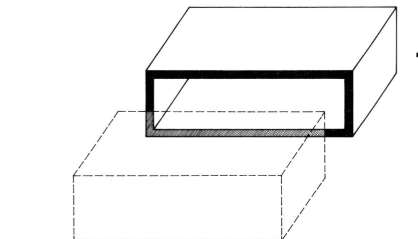

he other basic sectional cut is the longitudinal. This bisects a orm in a lengthwise direction.

.B.: Although one section drawing usually accounts for a cubic, ingle-cell building, a whole series of searching sections may be equired to expose the guts of more complex-shaped structures.

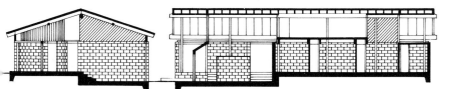

A-A

B-B

6

n order to help the iewer orientate, the recise location of ectional cuts should be learly indicated and nnotated on an accom- anying plan. The ends f section lines shown n plan often incorpor- te arrows that point in he direction of the view.

PLAN

7

By contrast to the exposure of contained space represented in the design section, the production section functions as a revelation of construction details within the thickness of the building fabric. Like their plan and elevation counter- parts, production sections are, essentially, diagrammatic drawings that use a language of graphic codes, symbols, and conventions to communicate to the contractor the buildability of a design scheme.

As part of a full set of working drawings that combine to convey a total picture of component, assembly, and locational information, key construction details are often drawn to a larger scale, such as 1/2" = 1' (1 : 20).

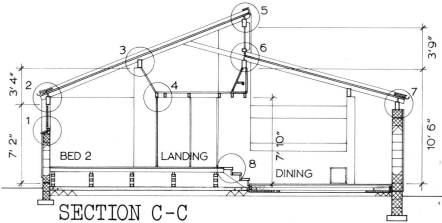

SECTION C-C

BED 2   LANDING   DINING

In seeking out typical construction details occurring at different spatial points in the plan, the trajectory of a production section line may be staggered, or jogged. However, the inquisitive route of a jogged section line must be clearly recorded and annotated on an accompanying plan.

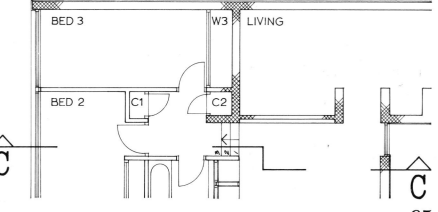

BED 3   W3   LIVING

BED 2   C1   C2

The Building Section

Not only does a design section expose interior space and the silhouette of the building profile along the line of the slice, but, in carving through both the building and the ground, its cut also describes the working relationship between a proposed architecture and the groundline. For example, a building may exist on, above, or below the groundline.

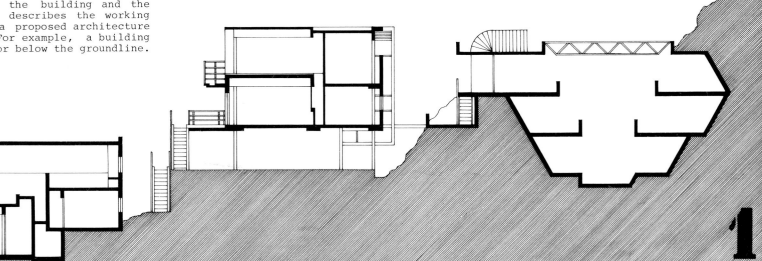

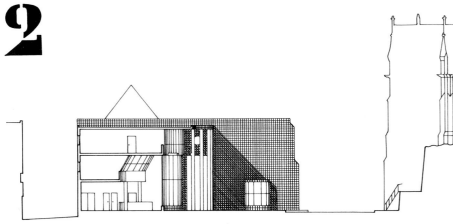

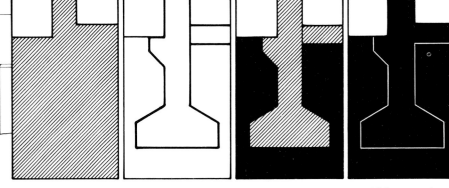

Apart from revealing interior spaces, sections that cut through selected parts of a more complex-shaped building form may maintain a view of unsliced facades that lay behind the cutting line.

N.B.: This simultaneous exposure of information seen within and without the cutaway area will appear as in elevation.

When drafting larger-scale sections, designers will occasionally show both construction details in walls, ceilings, and floors together with a pictorialized view of the interior. However, apart from the danger of confusion when combining design and production information, this does raise the issue of whether or not to depict a building section as "growing" from its groundline, i.e., minus its foundations as usually shown in design sections. Alternatively, it can be shown with its foundations profiled as an extension of the cut as it penetrates the groundmass.

The Sectional Elevation

1

There is no doubt that the section is a most satisfying graphic to draw; it certainly is one of the easiest. Here are some points to remember when drafting this peep-show graphic. The sectional elevation combines the view seen in a wall elevation (see page 48) as framed by the cutaway thickness of containing building fabric.

It is important to make sure that the sectional cut is dominant in the drawing. Confusion between the cut and other information is avoided by a clear depiction of its cutting edge. Depending on the scale and the medium used, the cut through the building and the ground plane can be contrasted with other detail by a use of black, white, or hatching, or be colored or picked out in dry transfer tone. This section is based on one by Ley Colbeck and Partners.

2

When section drawings are rendered exclusively in line, the profile of the cut (including the groundline) should be emphasized with a heavy line.

To imply depth, a decreasing line thickness can then be introduced to delineate progressively more distant objects from the point of the cut. The thinnest line should be reserved to indicate the end wall elevation. This section is based on a drawing by Robert Stern.

4

The "plinth" effect caused by the sectional slice through the ground plane helps to visually stabilize the composition of design sections. It also creates an ideal zone for the reception of lettering to label the drawing.

3

SECTION A-A

The Pictorial Potential of Sections

1 When a design section is drawn at a scale of 1/4" = 1' (1 : 50), and uses its cut to view the end wall of interiors, it provides the chance of exploring the textural effect of internal materials and their finishes. This section is based on a drawing by Robert Stern.

2

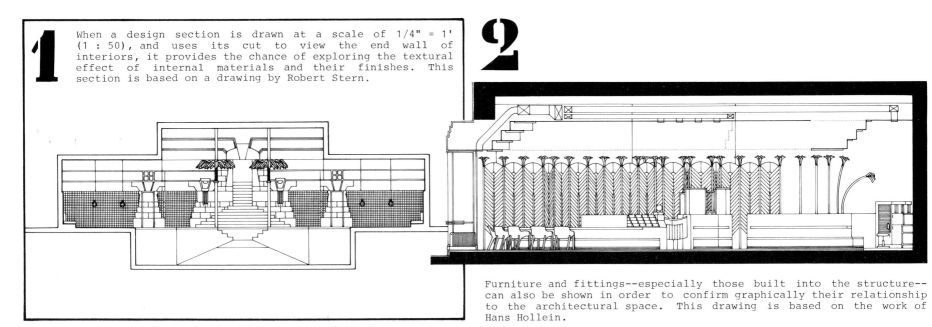

Furniture and fittings--especially those built into the structure-- can also be shown in order to confirm graphically their relationship to the architectural space. This drawing is based on the work of Hans Hollein.

3

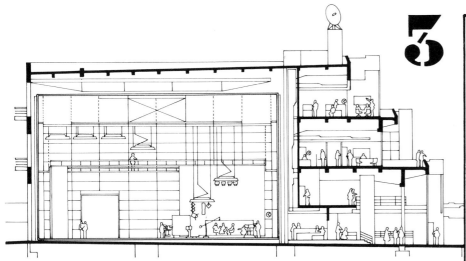

As always, the human figure will add that essential clue to scale in sections. A simple outline silhouette of a figure or a group of figures will help the viewer to identify with the nature of the interior presented. However, make sure that their presence does not impede the communication of architectural intent.

4

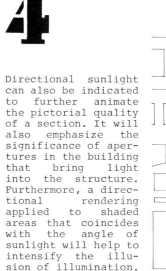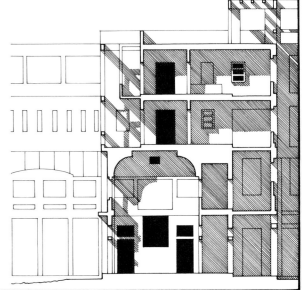

Directional sunlight can also be indicated to further animate the pictorial quality of a section. It will also emphasize the significance of apertures in the building that bring light into the structure. Furthermore, a directional rendering applied to shaded areas that coincides with the angle of sunlight will help to intensify the illusion of illumination.

The Pictorial Potential of Sections

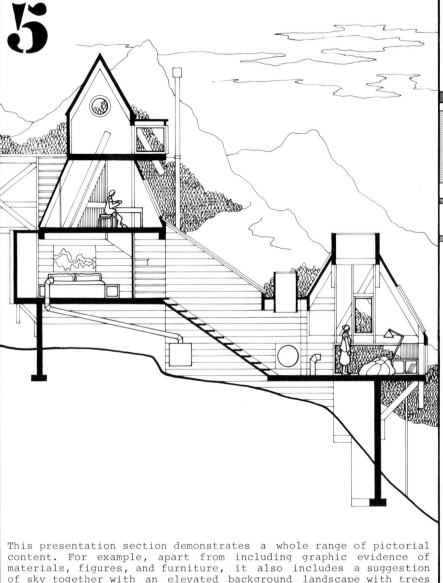

5

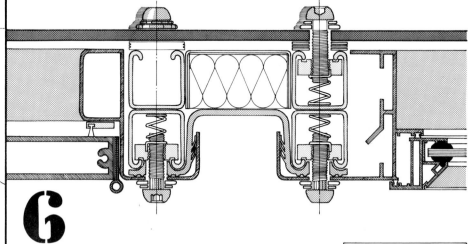

In complete contrast of scale, this working detail from an industrial building by Nicholas Grimshaw and Partners pictorializes elements to bring a greater sense of three dimensions to the image. Here, tonal value is used to indicate the effect of light and shade on bolts and, in the original drawing, colors applied by markers were added to code the various elements in the construction.

6

In windowless environments, or those with specific nighttime functions, interior electric lighting can be switched on graphically to illuminate the objects and activities of the interior section. Although the angles of light from illuminaires is often shown in line only, a supportive shading will help to increase the impact of any expressly directional lighting, such as in this section based on a sketch by Simon Dove.

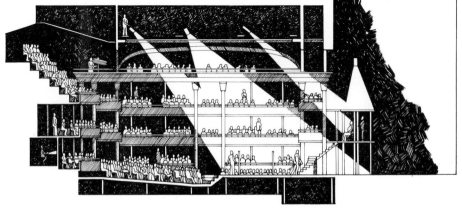

7

This presentation section demonstrates a whole range of pictorial content. For example, apart from including graphic evidence of materials, figures, and furniture, it also includes a suggestion of sky together with an elevated background landscape with trees to describe the topology of the site and its visual link, via windows, with the interior space.

The Site Section

1 The site section is an important design tool. Its function in site analysis can be experienced by making freehand sketch sections that trace the changing character along the point where physical mass meets the space above.

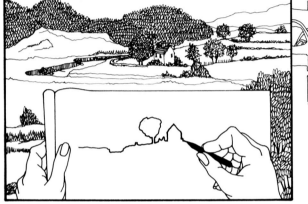

2 Another experience of the spatial role of the site section is gained from sketch-diagramming a series of diminishing sectional cuts through an urban or rural corridor. Each conceptual cut should record the edge of progressive planes that cut across your visual path.

3

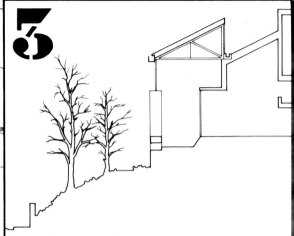

A further introductory project into the probing effect of site sections is to make a drawn slice through part of a building and progress its route out and into the surrounding space beyond its wall.

4

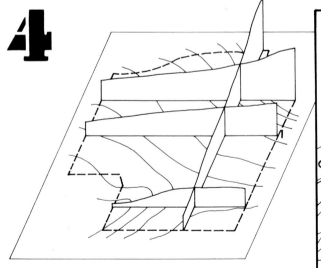

The role of the site section is related directly to that of the site plan. Together, they bring information to complete a three-dimensional picture of the area under study.

5 For instance, when a site survey plan is gridded, site sections can be made along representative grid lines. The sections are then annotated so that their location is clearly read on plan.

Section B

Section C

Section D

More specialized site sections can convey information concerning the geology of the landform, water tables, flood levels, and underground service systems. The site section format is also conducive to having supplementary written notes located above or below the line of the cut.

water table

springs

limestone outcrop

impervious clay strata

spring flood plain

maximum and minimum water table levels

6

RIVER.

The Site Section

Apart from its role in site analysis, the site section is also employed to convey the impact of a proposed design form on the wider context of its environment.

Urban site sections are also important in presentation as they expose the positive-negative relationship between inside and outside space as defined by existing and proposed form.

8

7

There are three potential types of site section: (A) the regular section, i.e., a line that simply delineates the contour of changing events along its route; (B) the sectional elevation, i.e., a section that includes in elevation events that lie behind and beyond its cut (see page 67); (C) the perspective section, i.e., a site section that uses a strategically positioned vanishing point to which all the forms along its cut are projected into three dimensions (see pages 72-74).

9

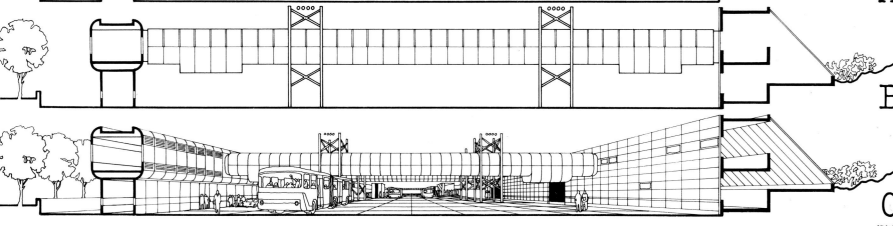

A

B

C

How to Set up a Perspective Section

1 The conversion of a section into a perspective section begins with a basically drafted scaled section--the location of its cut having responded to your predetermined idea of the view to be realized.

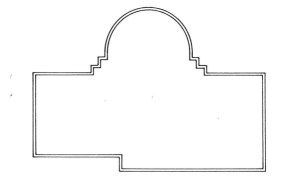

N.B.: The following are two methods of measuring depth in section-applied one-point perspective. Each method can be constructed on tracing paper taped over the section and later transferred into the drawing.

2 The section drawing functions as the picture plane, i.e., a true-to-scale framework through which the perspective will be projected and viewed. First, establish the horizon line (eye level) and the vanishing point (angle of view). Remember that a horizon line raised above scaled eye level will give added prominence to floor planes. Conversely, lowering the horizon line below scaled eye level will emphasize ceiling planes.

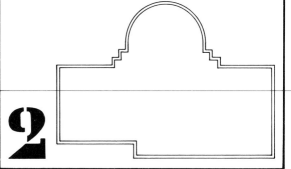

3

The vanishing point (VP) should be positioned on the horizon line to obtain the best possible angle of view. For instance, try locating the vanishing point off-center so that an important wall is emphasized. Once established, project lines from the vanishing point back to the inside corners of the section.

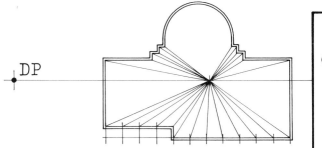

One method of constructing the perspective without the aid of a plan is to mark off increments of equal measure around the inner edge of the section and connect those on the floor plane back to the vanishing point. Then locate a diagonal point (DP) on the horizon line just outside the section.

N.B.: The distance between the diagonal point and the vanishing point should be at least as great as the width of the section.

5 The diagonal point represents the distance of the viewer from the picture plane (or section). The nearer its location to the vanishing point, the more acute the foreshortening in the resultant perspective. Now strike a line from the diagonal point to the farther, lower corner of the inside of the section.

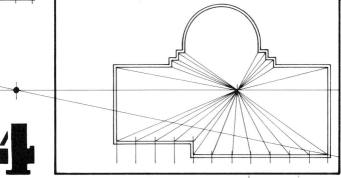

4

6 Where the diagonal line crosses the radiating floor plane lines establishes equal units of measure as diminishing in depth. These can now be easily projected around the walls and ceiling to guide the accurate location of the rear wall together with openings and objects in the interior space.

72

How to Set up a Perspective Section

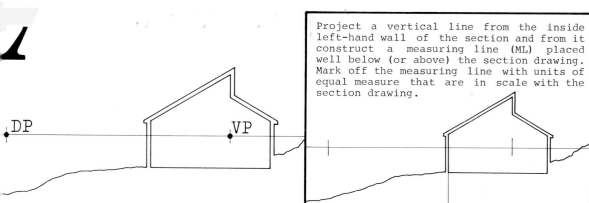

7

DP • VP

ere is another, more elegant method of
easuring depth in perspective sections. It
egins after the vanishing point (VP) and the
iagonal point (DP) are established on the
orizon line.

.B.: Remember to locate the diagonal point
ust outside the section at a distance from
he vanishing point not less than the width
f the section.

8

Project a vertical line from the inside
left-hand wall of the section and from it
construct a measuring line (ML) placed
well below (or above) the section drawing.
Mark off the measuring line with units of
equal measure that are in scale with the
section drawing.

ML ┤┼┼┼┼┼┼┼┼┼┼┼┼┼

9

From the point of intersection between the
vertical line and the measuring line, strike
a diagonal line to the vanishing point. The
corners of the space should also be connected
back to the vanishing point.

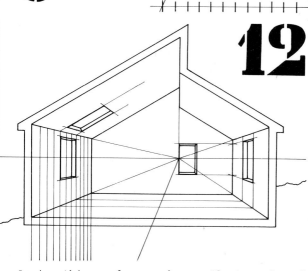

10

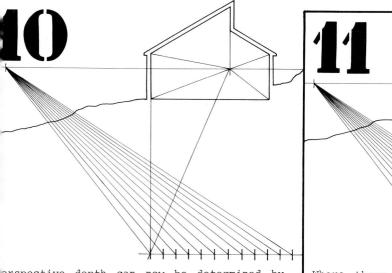

erspective depth can now be determined by
rojecting lines that radiate from the
iagonal point to bisect each of the units
arked on the measuring line.

11

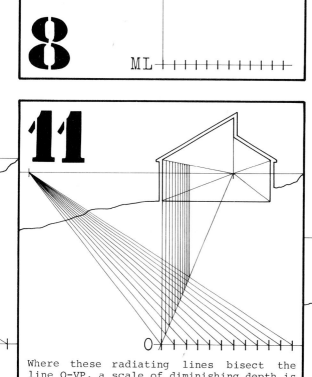

O ┤┼┼┼┼┼┼┼┼┼┼┼

Where these radiating lines bisect the
line O-VP, a scale of diminishing depth is
established.

12

Again, this scale can be easily transferred
around the horizontal and vertical planes of
the interior to construct a perspective grid
on which the room space can be accurately
delineated.

73

Setting up Multi-Cell Perspective Sections

Both the methods of constructing single-point perspective grids described on pages 72-73 are easily adaptable to the range of spaces contained by multi-cell perspective sections. In such cases, it is important to begin construction by spotting the vanishing point inside a main floor area or inside a central, major space, and on a horizon line at normal eye level.

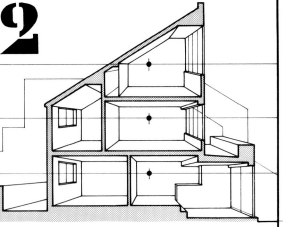

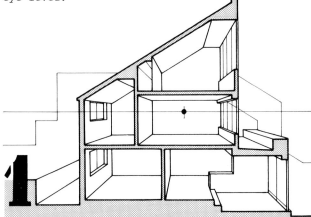

An alternative strategy for gaining an increased visual access into multi-cell perspective sections is to site vanishing points at the center of each floor of a multi-level building.

Another strategy is to place vanishing points inside individual spaces so that a personalized perspective view of each space is simultaneously presented. However, this type of drawing may produce an unwelcome distortion.

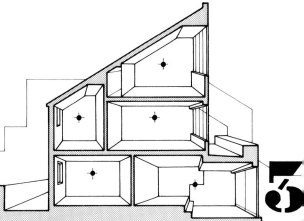

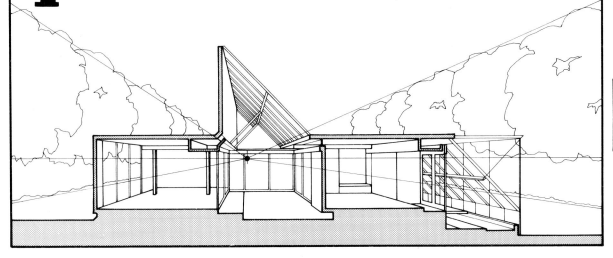

4 Using the coordinates already established in the single-point perspective, the opportunity arises of accurately including contextual site information that may occur to either side of the building. As a basic rule, this kind of detail should be rendered minimally so as not to present a visual distraction.

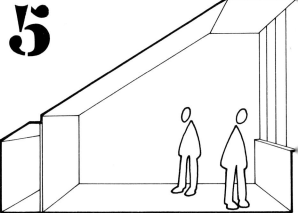

Furthermore, it is also wise to keep newly drawn interiors free from unnecessary clutter so that relationships between interior spaces remain the dominant message of the drawing. However, simply drawn or dry transfer scale figures inserted into the various spaces can populate the building with a sense of scale and life.

Various Building Sections in Action

Another, more unusual version of the perspective section is one involving two vanishing points. Two-point perspective sections are rarely seen but can be used to create a visual that, although orthographically distorted, can convey a sense of dynamism as well as accent a particular interior area by its direction of view (two-point perspective is covered on pages 105-127).

Possibly the greatest promoter and exponent of the architectural section is Paul Rudolph--the open and cellular nature of his buildings seeming inextricably linked to their cutting action. Furthermore, Rudolph's use of pen hatching appears to transcend mechanical line work to produce scintillating atmospheric effects. This drawing is based on a detail of one of his works.

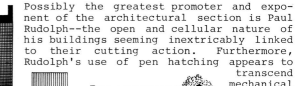

This section is animated by directional symbols in order to function as a working diagram that explains the effect of solar heating and cooling on a building design. As a mechanism, the section is often employed to test the dynamics of a new idea at birth as well as convey their resolution in presentation form to others.

When applied to axonometrics, the section can easily travel in three dimensions in response to the kind of view that is required to be exposed. As always, the route and thickness of its cut should be clearly depicted, such as in this drawing derived from the work of Levitt Bernstein Associates (axonometric projection drawing is covered on pages 83-104).

Techniques for Rendering Sections

1 An ink drawing of a perspective section on transparent or opaque paper can be given an added depth dimension by the application of three or four tones of dry transfer screens. For example, a dark tone used for the areas of sectional cut combined with a mid-gray tone on rear interior walls will appear to flood rooms with a glowing light.

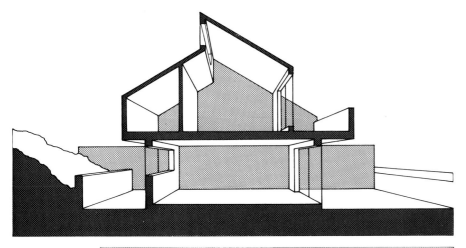

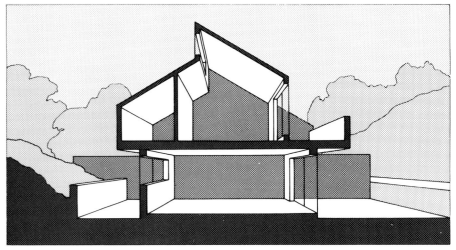

2 In directing the viewer to interior cells, this apparent illumination is emphasized by the use of a light tone for the sky area together with a slightly darker shade for areas of site context, background, and skyline.

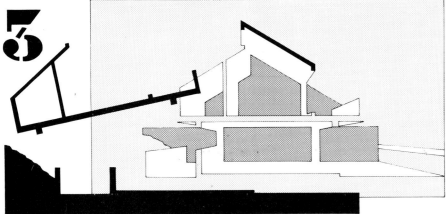

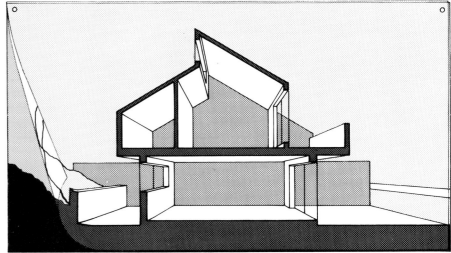

3 An alternative method for achieving this illusion of a glowing effect applies to perspective sections drawn in line on tracing paper. For this technique, tone is applied to a backing sheet as paint or as a collage comprising white, black, and mid-gray papers. These basic tones are organized around an outline tracing made from the original drawing: black representing sectional cut, white representing interior spaces, and mid-gray representing sky area and any parts of the building not shown in section.

4 The tracing paper line drawing is then superimposed over the backing-sheet for presentation, the supporting tones being viewed through the upper transparent layer.

Techniques for Rendering Sections

Pen and ink hatching techniques also work well in perspective sections. This is because, being governed by the vanishing point, the technique can appear as directional--hatched lines reinforcing the illusion of depth. Several means of deploying tonal value are open to the designer. One has already been described, i.e., the application of a mid-tone hatching to rear walls in combination with a heavily hatched sectional cut.

6 Another is to establish a tonal equilibrium for the drawing: dark tones for floor planes, mid-tones for wall planes, and light tones for ceiling planes. Depending on the scale of the drawing, this technique may either elaborate or ignore the modular units of surface materials as seen in perspective.

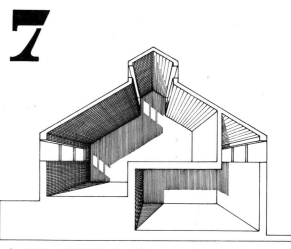

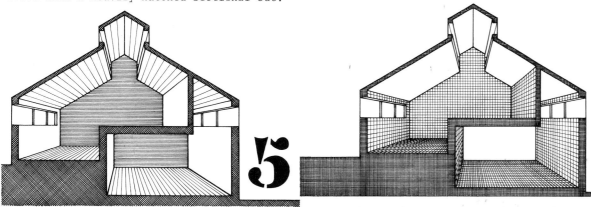

A more pictorial version of the hatching technique can assume sunlight streaming into rooms through side windows and the sectional cut, its direction casting shadows that function to hollow out the exposed view of their spaces.

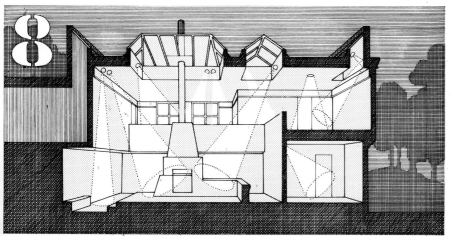

However, one of the best methods for showing the interiors of perspective sections is to present them as after-dark settings, i.e., rendering the area surrounding the building section as slightly lighter in value than the black of the sectional cut. Then graphically "switching on" all the internal electric lights highlights a sharp contrast between "inside" and "outside."

9 In larger-scale sections that contain built-in furniture and fittings, a hatching technique might concentrate solely on describing the texture of their surface finishes against the more passive rendering of structural planes.

N.B.: Some of the techniques for simulating materials in elevations described on pages 40-45 can be adapted to this particular kind of interior design section.

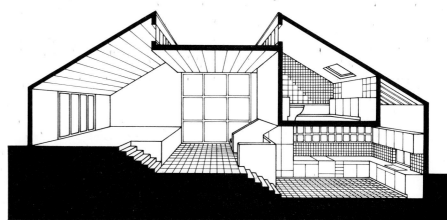

Hybrid and Specialized Graphics

The section is often used in the intimate company of a part elevation to provide a penetrating, double-vision impression of the inner and outer workings of a built form. Here is such a drawing that discloses simultaneously information about the inside and outside of a structure.

Here is another specialized part section, part elevation--this time used to combine a glimpse of the interior spaces of a structure with a view of its external appearance. This drawing is based on the work of John Potter.

The direct working relationship between the horizontal section--in the form of the plan-- and the vertical section is also common, as it provides a clear visual cross-reference between the two spatial types of information.

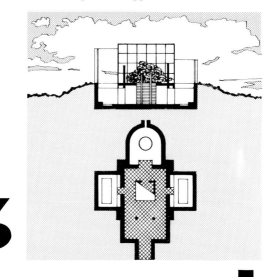

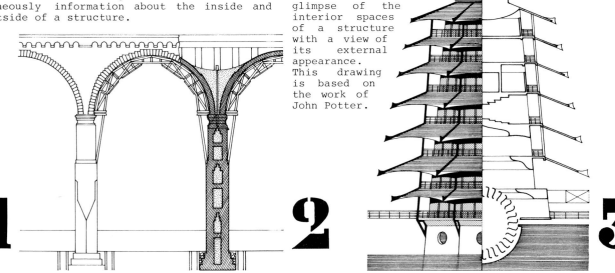

The hybrid combination of the section and the elevation is useful when explaining both the method of construction and the design intention, such as in this part elevation, part "skin-deep" section (or unclad elevation) derived from a drawing by the Nicholas Grimshaw design office. Such drawings underline the direct relationship between "design" and "construction"-- the integrated disciplines of design occasionally separated artificially in the mind of some designers.

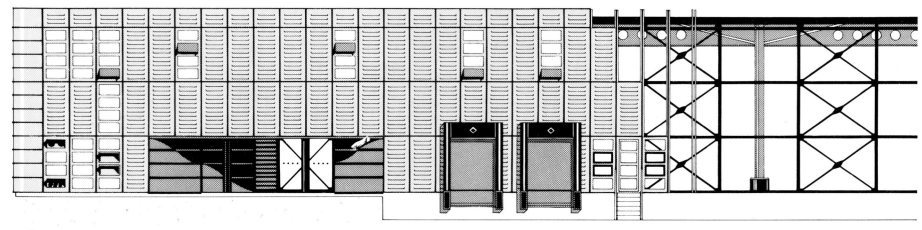

Hybrid and Specialized Graphics

5 The use of mixtures of graphic types in newspaper visuals makes an interesting study as they often incorporate the plan, elevation, and section together with photography and other graphic modes to illustrate events in space and time. This artwork combines the "plan" with a perspective--represented by a photograph--and a superimposed section. While the inset map provides the location and number of blast furnaces in the United Kingdom, the section explains the operation of a blast furnace--the main message of the graphic being the indication of danger points in the process. Notice the way that the labels are clearly depicted, and that the key labels are reversed for extra visual punch, i.e., shown as white lettering on a black background.

This composite graphic again uses a photograph to set the scene on which a section is superimposed to bring diagrammatic information concerning the physical extent of the remains of a newly discovered wreck. The section also brings information about the process of excavation and its apparatus together with the effect in time of tidal movement. In order to utilize the multi-view of a three-dimensional graphic, the section has been projected back into the space of an axonometric oblique drawing (axonometrics are discussed on pages 84-104).

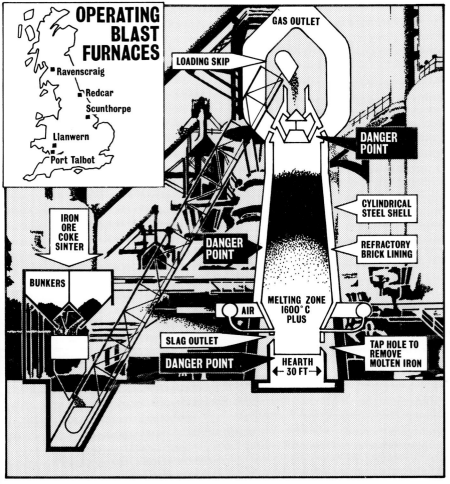

OPERATING BLAST FURNACES

- Ravenscraig
- Redcar
- Scunthorpe
- Llanwern
- Port Talbot

GAS OUTLET

LOADING SKIP

DANGER POINT

CYLINDRICAL STEEL SHELL

REFRACTORY BRICK LINING

IRON ORE COKE SINTER

DANGER POINT

BUNKERS

MELTING ZONE 1600°C PLUS

AIR

SLAG OUTLET

DANGER POINT

HEARTH ← 30 FT →

TAP HOLE TO REMOVE MOLTEN IRON

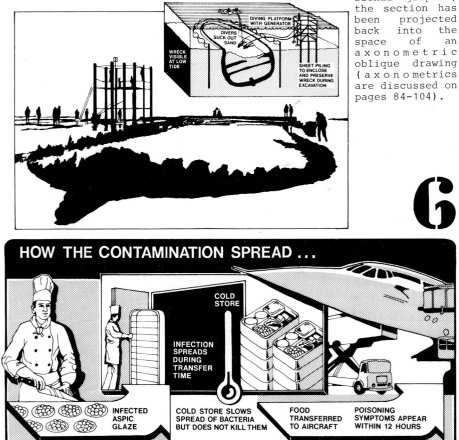

DIVING PLATFORM WITH GENERATOR

DIVERS SUCK OUT SAND

WRECK VISIBLE AT LOW TIDE

SHEET PILING TO ENCLOSE AND PRESERVE WRECK DURING EXCAVATION

6

HOW THE CONTAMINATION SPREAD ...

COLD STORE

INFECTION SPREADS DURING TRANSFER TIME

INFECTED ASPIC GLAZE

COLD STORE SLOWS SPREAD OF BACTERIA BUT DOES NOT KILL THEM

FOOD TRANSFERRED TO AIRCRAFT

POISONING SYMPTOMS APPEAR WITHIN 12 HOURS

7 This artwork illustrates how a collection of graphic components can be assembled to communicate a complex chain of related events. Here, the various directions and scale of viewpoint have been exercised to alternate along spatial and schematic stages. Notice that in the final stage of the sequence the deeper space implied by the perspective is linked back into the foreground by overlapping the nose of the aeroplane on the inset drawing. Perspective is discussed on pages 106-127.

Basic Orthographic Presentation

1 In design presentation, the respective viewpoints of orthographics each play a coordinating role in a spatial narrative. For example, the progressively descending scales of the location plan, neighborhood plan, and the site plan, traditionally introduce and orientate the viewer who, from an overhead viewpoint, "arrives" on the site for a closer analysis of its nature via diagrams, sketches, sections, and so on.

2 An important link in presentation between the results of a site analysis and the ensuing design is the diagramming of the design strategy.

N.B.: To avoid confusion, all plans along the sequence of presentation should be shown with the same orientation. Traditionally, these are coordinated with their north points in an upward position.

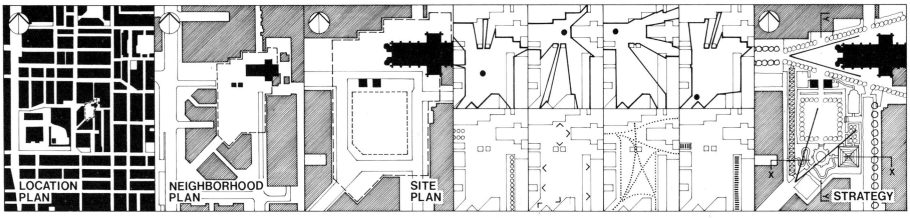

LOCATION PLAN

NEIGHBORHOOD PLAN

SITE PLAN

STRATEGY

The design proposal is then presented via the overhead view offered by the plan that, operating as a horizontal section, slices the form at key levels. These are coordinated in scale and, either horizontally or vertically, related directly to the head-on views of the external appearance and internal workings offered respectively by the elevation and the section. When more than one storey is involved, floorplans should be vertically or horizontally stacked.

3 The site section moves the spectator's viewpoint horizontally away for a more distant and sliced impression of the impact of the form on the surrounding environment. The opportunity for contextual presentation is provided when a ground floor plan is shown directly on a site plan, and when elevations embrace events beyond the face of the form they portray.

4 All the drawing modes discussed thus far have been graphics that rely upon their counterparts in order to allow the viewer to "reconstruct" a three-dimensional idea. However, there are two further drawing types that offer a graphic summary of a design concept and they would normally occupy the final stage of a presentation sequence. These are represented by axonometric and isometric projection and perspective. They are discussed respectively in the following chapters.

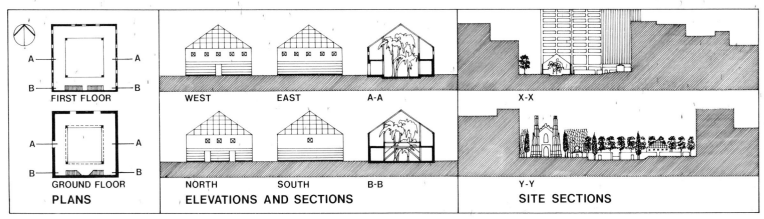

FIRST FLOOR

GROUND FLOOR

PLANS

WEST   EAST   A-A

NORTH   SOUTH   B-B

ELEVATIONS AND SECTIONS

X-X

Y-Y

SITE SECTIONS

Traditional and Experimental Layouts

1

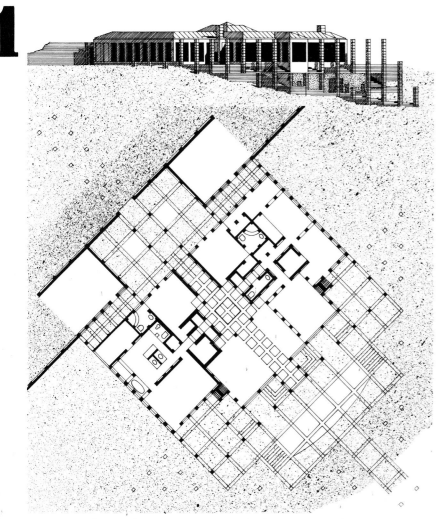

The various orthographic components of a traditional presentation layout can often appear to float aimlessly around the sheet on which they are drafted. However, the potential sparseness of this plan-related elevation has been overcome by the use of spray pigment. Rather than function merely as a blank background to the two orthographic views, the sheet has been considered as an entity with each drawing appearing to occupy its own space. Notice the clear hierarchy of information that is conveyed by the plan together with the powerful sense of space around an elevation that sports both texture and light, shade, and shadow. This is based on a drawing by Batey & Mack.

2

The upsurge in the number of design competitions and their attendant restriction on both the size and amount of submitted sheets has led to much experiment in the manner in which the various orthographic elements may be related for presentation. For example, this is one sheet layout taken from a competition entry by the Building Design Partnership. Here, elevations, drawn at two scales, a part plan, and a section are tightly juxtaposed to utilize every inch of the format.

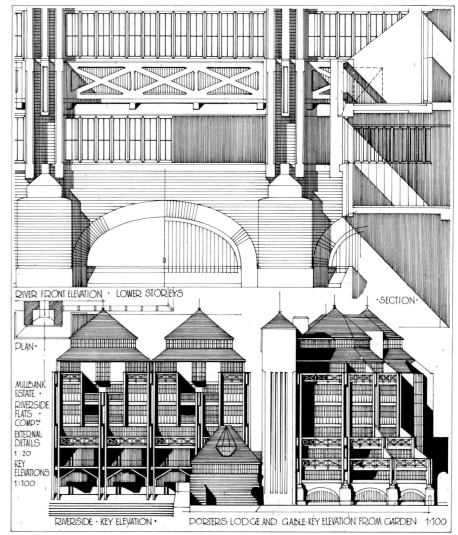

RIVER FRONT ELEVATION · LOWER STOREYS

·SECTION·

PLAN·

MILLBANK ESTATE · RIVERSIDE FLATS · COMP^N EXTERNAL DETAILS 1:20 KEY ELEVATIONS 1:100

RIVERSIDE · KEY ELEVATION ·

PORTERS LODGE AND GABLE KEY ELEVATION FROM GARDEN 1:100

Experimental Layouts

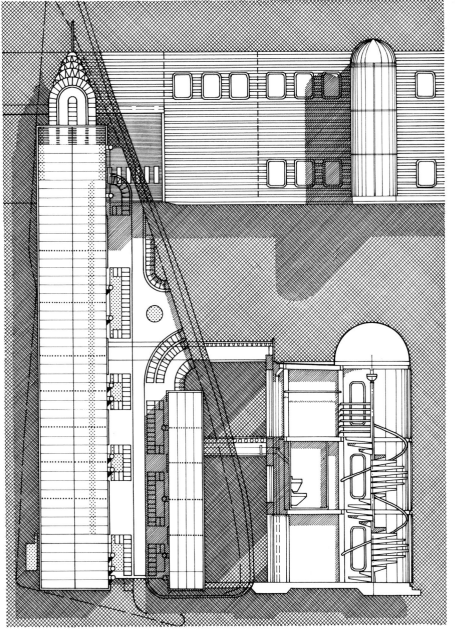

1 The more experimental relationship between various orthographic types has led to some interesting, if not curious, drawings. For example, this drawing on the left (after one by David Richmond) brings together the section, elevation, and roof plan of Nicholas Grimshaw and Partners Advanced Industrial Units at Nottingham and assembles them into a Constructivist-type statement.

2 This experimental drawing below combines a whole range of orthographic views including section, plan, elevation, and isometric planes into a closer fusion of spatial information. This almost Cubist-like attempt to graphically summarize the totality of a design idea is taken from the work of Pedro Guedes.

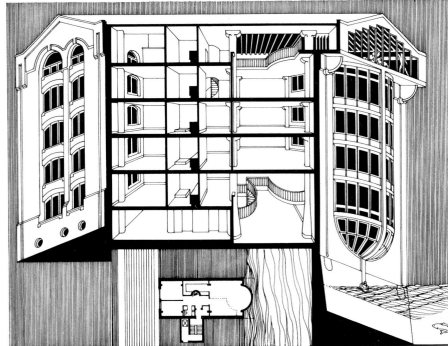

4 AXONOMETRICS AND ISOMETRICS

Introducing the Axonometric

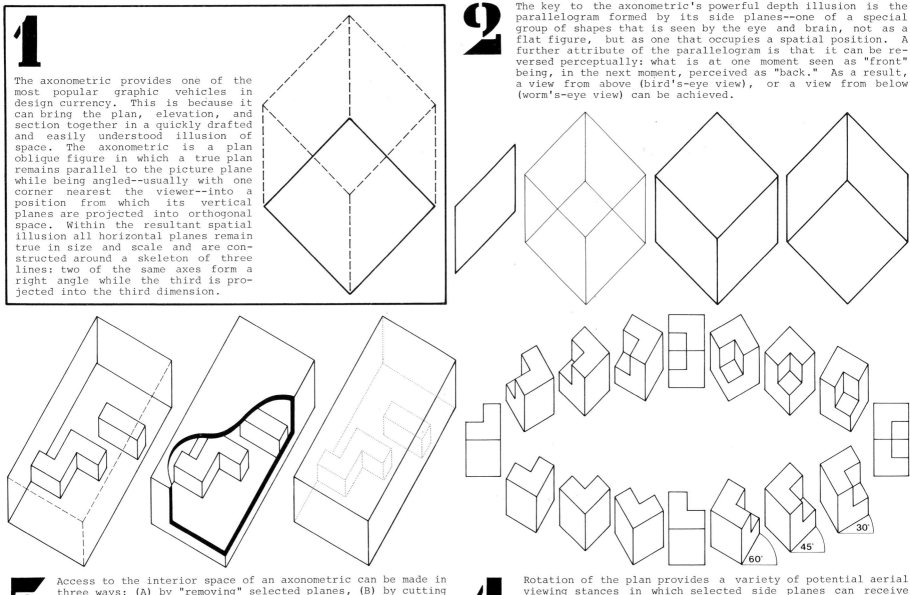

1 The axonometric provides one of the most popular graphic vehicles in design currency. This is because it can bring the plan, elevation, and section together in a quickly drafted and easily understood illusion of space. The axonometric is a plan oblique figure in which a true plan remains parallel to the picture plane while being angled--usually with one corner nearest the viewer--into a position from which its vertical planes are projected into orthogonal space. Within the resultant spatial illusion all horizontal planes remain true in size and scale and are constructed around a skeleton of three lines: two of the same axes form a right angle while the third is projected into the third dimension.

2 The key to the axonometric's powerful depth illusion is the parallelogram formed by its side planes--one of a special group of shapes that is seen by the eye and brain, not as a flat figure, but as one that occupies a spatial position. A further attribute of the parallelogram is that it can be reversed perceptually: what is at one moment seen as "front" being, in the next moment, perceived as "back." As a result, a view from above (bird's-eye view), or a view from below (worm's-eye view) can be achieved.

3 Access to the interior space of an axonometric can be made in three ways: (A) by "removing" selected planes, (B) by cutting a visual hole around the area of interest, or (C) by "dissolving" opaque and intermediate planes to produce a see-through revelation.

4 Rotation of the plan provides a variety of potential aerial viewing stances in which selected side planes can receive different degrees of emphasis. The plan orientations shown here represent those most commonly used in architectural and interior design.

84

Introducing the Isometric

By contrast to the axonometric, the iso-metric figure responds to a viewpoint that is lower in relation to the groundplane. This is because its plan is tilted and seen as a foreshortened plane--the two true-length groundplane axes being both angled at 30 degrees above the horizontal.

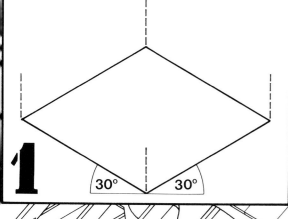

1

30°　30°

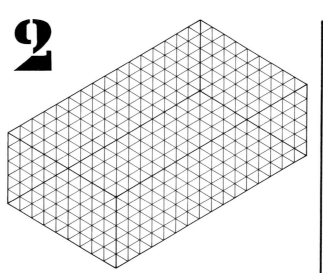

2

Meanwhile, the height axis is represented by a vertical line and the height of the verti-cal dimension remains constant throughout the space occupied by the figure.

When constructing an isometric begin by drafting the three major axes. When laying out isometric lines, make measurements only along routes parallel to the three principal axes and use the same architec-tural scale in each of the three direc-tions.

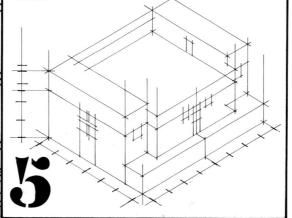

5

3

As the isometric figure presents more overall surface area than, for example, a perspective figure, this graphic mode can prove very useful when conveying large amounts of complex detail about a form or a plane within a small amount of format.

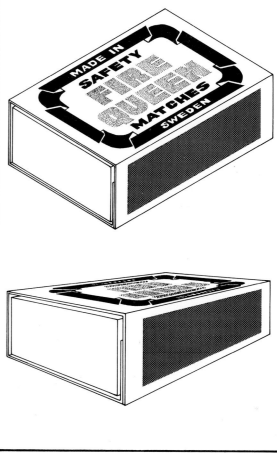

4

For example, by substituting length and width for depth, isometric planes are ideal when it becomes necessary to communicate layers of precise information.

Isometrics in Action

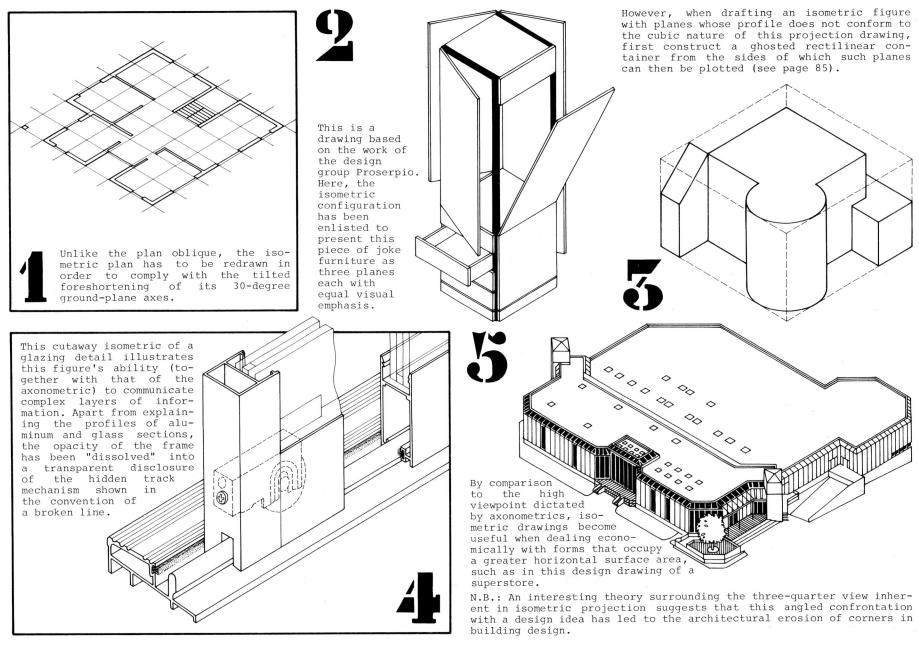

1 Unlike the plan oblique, the isometric plan has to be redrawn in order to comply with the tilted foreshortening of its 30-degree ground-plane axes.

2 This is a drawing based on the work of the design group Proserpio. Here, the isometric configuration has been enlisted to present this piece of joke furniture as three planes each with equal visual emphasis.

However, when drafting an isometric figure with planes whose profile does not conform to the cubic nature of this projection drawing, first construct a ghosted rectilinear container from the sides of which such planes can then be plotted (see page 85).

3

4 This cutaway isometric of a glazing detail illustrates this figure's ability (together with that of the axonometric) to communicate complex layers of information. Apart from explaining the profiles of aluminum and glass sections, the opacity of the frame has been "dissolved" into a transparent disclosure of the hidden track mechanism shown in the convention of a broken line.

5 By comparison to the high viewpoint dictated by axonometrics, isometric drawings become useful when dealing economically with forms that occupy a greater horizontal surface area, such as in this design drawing of a superstore.

N.B.: An interesting theory surrounding the three-quarter view inherent in isometric projection suggests that this angled confrontation with a design idea has led to the architectural erosion of corners in building design.

Isometrics in Action

This is a classic interior isometric drawing derived from that produced by Herbert Bayer in 1923. Here, the ruthless articulation of interior forms is at one with the "glass box" coordinates of the isometric figure. This drawing appears to represent a "chicken-and-egg" situation, i.e., whether the interior has been contained by the isometric, or whether the isometric container has determined the interior design. For instance, notice how every element in this space appears fixed and fashioned by an invisible grid--the force of which apparently controlling even the design of light fittings and carpet pattern.

7

6

This cutaway office interior isometric has been redrawn as an axonometric for the purpose of a direct comparison between the two modes of projection drawing. Quite apart from the obvious differences in each view caused by the higher viewpoint emanating from the true-plan, and the lower viewpoint given by the tilted and distorted isometric plan, both axonometric and isometric provide highly realistic impressions of interior space. By lifting away the top and side planes, they both convert the plan into an image that is instantly recognizable to any viewer. Furthermore, both projection drawings appear as a kind of two-point perspective in which the vanishing points are at infinity.

How to Construct an Axonometric

1

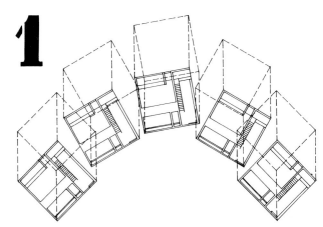

Drafting an axonometric of a cubic form is both simple and fast. However, an early decision concerns the best angle from which to view the figure in response to the kind of information that is to be conveyed. This is done by rotating the plan to determine the most convenient angle whilst mentally projecting its vertical planes.

2

Although the plan can be rescaled and redrafted on opaque drawing material, the method of direct plan projection is quickest. To do this, tape the plan positioned in its required projection angle on the drawing board and superimpose a taped sheet of transparent drawing material.

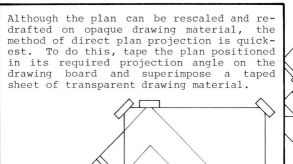

3

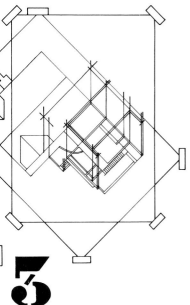

After checking that the ensuing projection will fit comfortably within the format of the overlay, extrude the corners of all the plan's vertical receding planes parallel to the selected angle of projection and to the height determined by the architectural scale in use. Start by drafting the elements at the front of the image so as not to waste time by drawing parts that will be hidden from view.

4

If the axonometric conversion of the plan produces an over-elongated impression of the vertical planes, the height scale ratio can be proportionally reduced. Although sacrificing dimensional consistency, this foreshortening--when applied--usually shrinks the vertical scale by one-half or one-quarter.

5

Once the basic framework is established, any point can now be plotted within the space contained by the axonometric. This is because scale and size ratios remain constant in all horizontal and vertical planes.

6

Also, shapes that appear within the diagonal distortion of the side planes not parallel to the picture plane are easily plotted.

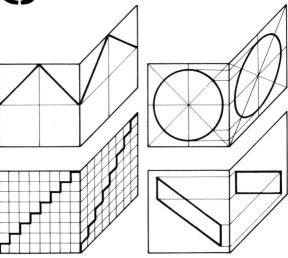

How to Construct an Axonometric

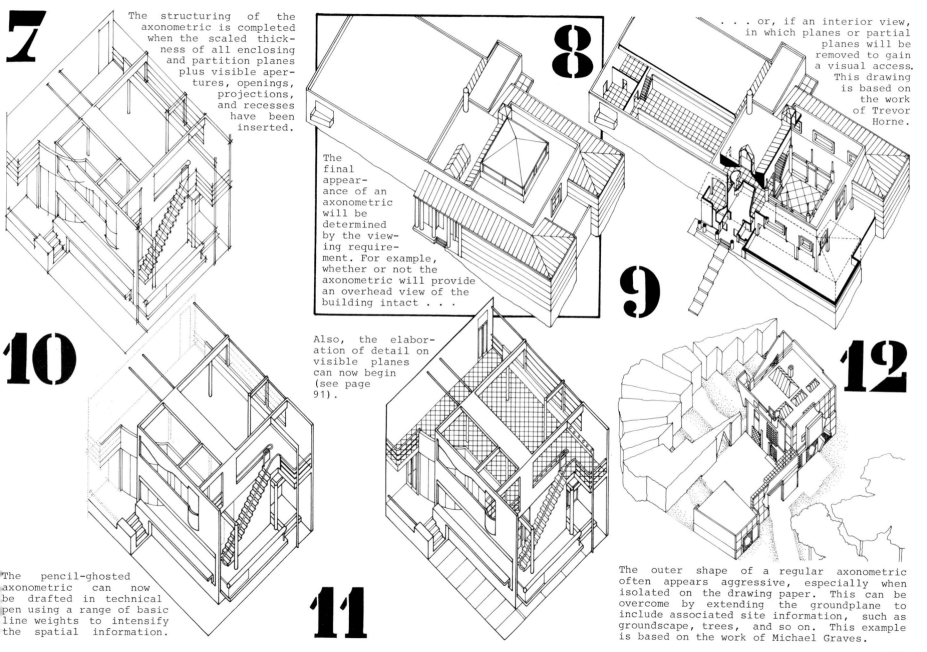

7 The structuring of the axonometric is completed when the scaled thickness of all enclosing and partition planes plus visible apertures, openings, projections, and recesses have been inserted.

8 The final appearance of an axonometric will be determined by the viewing requirement. For example, whether or not the axonometric will provide an overhead view of the building intact . . .

9 . . . or, if an interior view, in which planes or partial planes will be removed to gain a visual access. This drawing is based on the work of Trevor Horne.

10 Also, the elaboration of detail on visible planes can now begin (see page 91).

11 The pencil-ghosted axonometric can now be drafted in technical pen using a range of basic line weights to intensify the spatial information.

12 The outer shape of a regular axonometric often appears aggressive, especially when isolated on the drawing paper. This can be overcome by extending the groundplane to include associated site information, such as groundscape, trees, and so on. This example is based on the work of Michael Graves.

Tips When Constructing Axonometrics

1 Whenever floor and roof plans are available there are a number of tips that can facilitate the construction of more complex axonometric forms using the plans as underlays. When using this method the underlay plan is relocated at various levels and the visible edges of elements are projected downward (rather than upward as in the method described on pages 88-89).

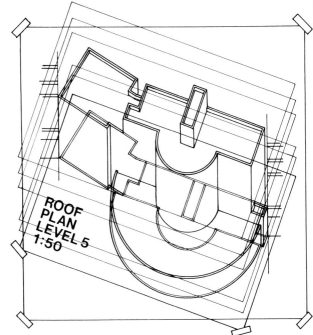

ROOF
PLAN
LEVEL 5
1:50

To construct an axonometric of the external form of a complex building, the basic form can be extruded using the roof plan as an underlay. First position the plan at the angle required near the top of the sheet. Next construct measuring lines in pencil on the overlay sheet to either side of the plan --marking on parapet, roof, and ground levels. Check that the "nearest" part of the plan will not overshoot the bottom edge of the sheet. Start by drafting the uppermost part of the roof plan. Then, level by level, slide the underlay down, drafting in the roof elements as they occur and projecting vertical forms downward to meet the floor plan.

2

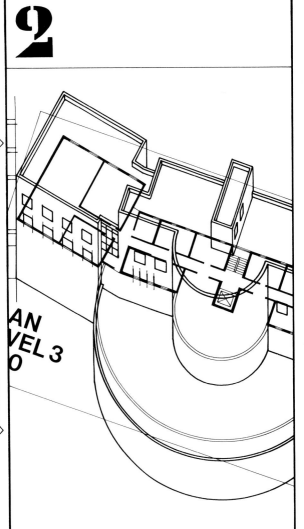

AN
VEL 3
0

Once the basic form has been drafted, the floor plans can be introduced as underlays to locate fenestration, exposed floor patterns, and so on. Finally, if a same-size site plan is available, external groundscape features can be added.

3 A similar method can be used for axonometrics that cut away roof planes to expose the interior. Obviously, this is easier when the walls of a building design are all at the same height and the floor is at one level. First draft the basic outline of the plan, then slide the plan downward to the required height and project downward all visible planes.

When wall and floor heights vary, construct measuring lines to either side of the plan. Starting at the top, next draw in the visible elements level by level before projecting the vertical edges of forms to connect the levels. Finally, add elevational details. The example shown is also based on a design by Michael Graves.

The Plan Oblique: Vertical Projection

All the axonometric drawings on this page rotate their true-shape plans before projecting their receding planes vertically into the space created by this graphic. This axonometric uses its plan as a "plinth" on which the projected planes of an exhibition layout are presented as three planes of equal information.

This interior design of a shop based on a drawing by Mark Lintott is positioned at 45 degrees to the horizontal. However, the roof plane has been "removed" to reveal the elevated position of the plan through which clothesracks, rear changing rooms, and suspended ceiling are seen, but allowing the front facade to over-reach its cut and achieve its full height. The decision to swing the plan to the right rather than the left was made by the need to show the basement staircase.

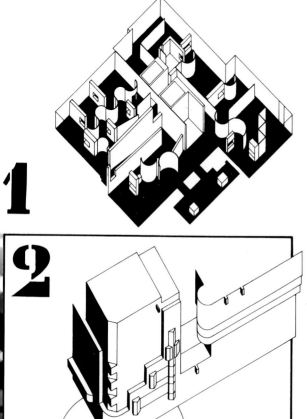

1

2

On the other hand, this projection drawing of a building exterior rotates its plan into 30-degree and 60-degree angles to the horizontal in order to present two unequal vertical planes plus roof to examine in an economical way the articulation of a corner facade.

3

4

This axonometric swings to the left into a 60-degree angle on its long facade to provide a sophisticated series of dissecting views. These take us from interior glimpse (center portion) to roof construction (rear portion) to an appreciation of the completed and cladded form (near portion). Notice the use of "hidden lines" to ghost the partition wall behind the near, roofed section.

The Planometric

1

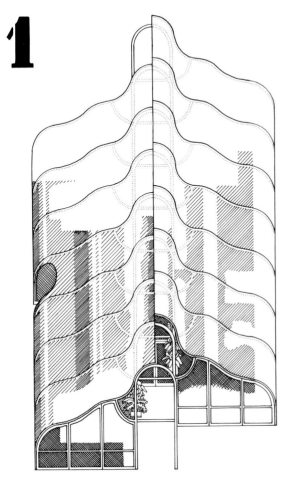

This unusual version of the axonometric extrudes vertically the receding planes of a true plan positioned with one of its sides parallel to the picture plane. By abandoning the ability to describe right-angled side planes, this form of projection also loses any convincing evidence of the third dimension. However, despite this distortion, this pictorial mode finds popularity among many leading designers.

For example, in this drawing based on the work of the Terry Farrell design group, the cascading glass form is adequately described by the planometric.

2

However, with rectilinear form distortion increases and is only relieved by elements that run contrary to the squareness of a cubic form.

This student drawing by Kumi-Fukuhara of the Chelsea School of Art studies furniture layout and circulation after a "removal" of the near wall and ceiling planes. Notice how the plan remains virtually intact except for its extension to gain a glimpse of the lower floor. Also notice how the height of the upper floor is implied by the indication of the change in plane made within the thickness of its walls.

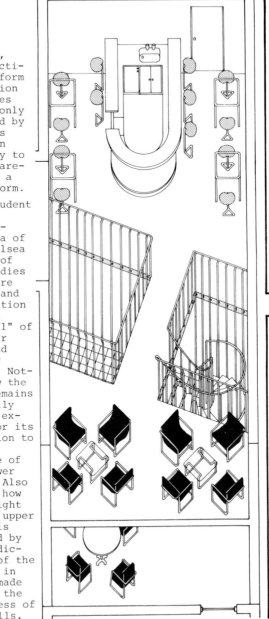

3

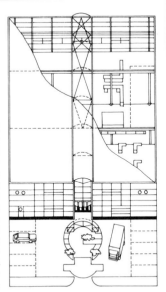

Partial views of roof and interior are projected within the confines of this vertical plan projection -- also based on the work of Terry Farrell. Furthermore, the drawing takes advantage of relating the front facade with the forecourt layout.

4

By producing a simultaneous view of facade and roofscape within a vertical projection of a right-angled plan, this drawing demonstrates the inherent flattening illusion of the planometric -- a distortion in which the roof plane appears tilted toward the viewer.

The Plan Oblique: Near-Vertical Projection

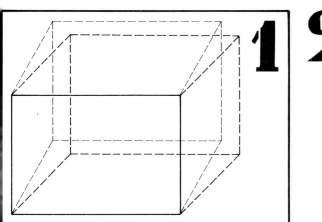

1

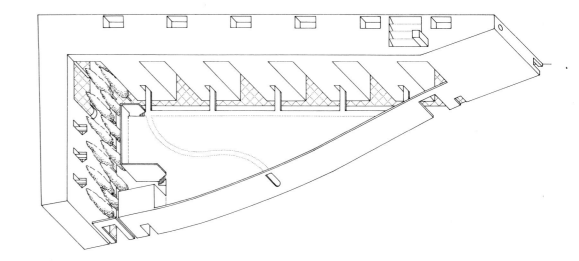

2

The plan oblique projection drawing can also angle its upright planes so that they lie parallel in a near-vertical direction. The resulting axonometric container conceptually flies the designer into a viewing stance that is positioned almost directly above a design idea.

To achieve this vantage point, the extruded and vertical planes of true-plans are projected upward at an angle, usually 45 degrees or 60 degrees. As always in axonometrics, the option of swinging vertical planes to the left or to the right--or upward or downward--will depend on the viewing requirements.

3

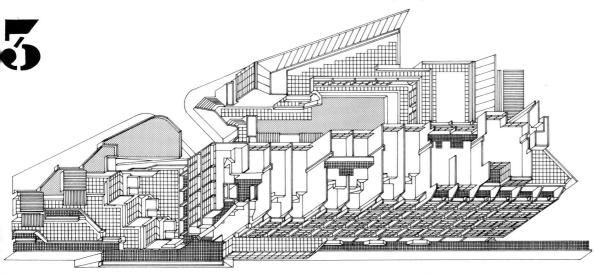

4

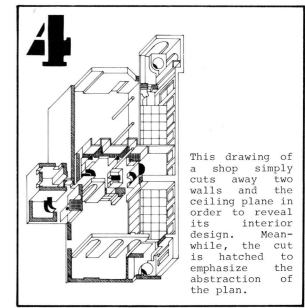

The salient feature of this projection drawing is that the near-overhead location of its viewpoint causes vertical planes--together with the information they carry--to foreshorten. This distortion makes way for a reasonably unimpeded view that can concentrate on external and internal horizontal planes, as in this projection based on the work of Evans and Shalev.

This drawing of a shop simply cuts away two walls and the ceiling plane in order to reveal its interior design. Meanwhile, the cut is hatched to emphasize the abstraction of the plan.

The Elevation Oblique

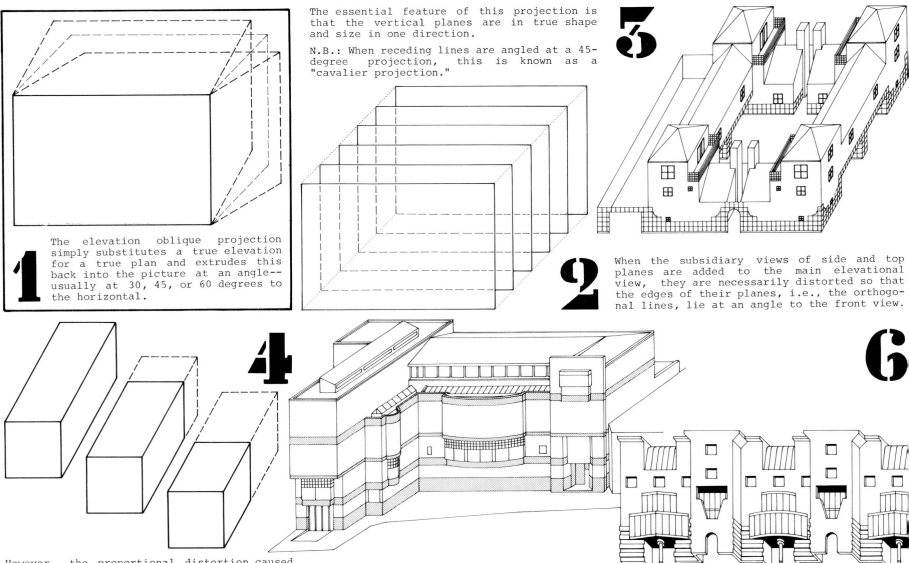

The essential feature of this projection is that the vertical planes are in true shape and size in one direction.

N.B.: When receding lines are angled at a 45-degree projection, this is known as a "cavalier projection."

1 The elevation oblique projection simply substitutes a true elevation for a true plan and extrudes this back into the picture at an angle-- usually at 30, 45, or 60 degrees to the horizontal.

2 When the subsidiary views of side and top planes are added to the main elevational view, they are necessarily distorted so that the edges of their planes, i.e., the orthogonal lines, lie at an angle to the front view.

4 However, the proportional distortion caused by the projection of true-length orthogonal lines can, to an extent, be adjusted. One adjustment is the general oblique that reduces the receding planes by one-quarter; another adjustment is the cabinet oblique that reduces the receding planes by one-half.

5 The elevation oblique is usually employed to depict the longest side of an object or a building, or the side with the most irregular shape. This drawing is based on the work of Colquhoun and Miller.

6 The ever-present option of producing a worm's-eye view is illustrated by this elevation oblique of a "floating" facade based on the work of James Stirling, Michael Wilford, and Associates.

How to Construct Ellipses and Cylinders

1

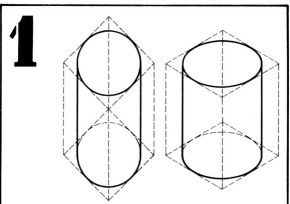

As circles in axonometric projection drawings retain their true-plan shape and size, they are drafted quickly and directly with the aid of a compass for an extrusion into cylindrical forms. On the other hand, as circles in the distortion of isometric planes appear as ellipses, they require some preparatory construction.

The construction of an ellipse begins with two pairs of radiating lines, each pair springing from the near and far corners of the isometric square at 60 degrees to the horizontal to bisect each of its sides.

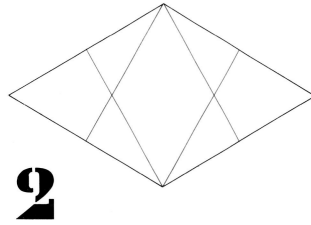

2

Points C and D then become the centers for two further arcs that complete the ellipse by establishing the curves that occupy the obtuse corners of the isometric square.

3

Points A and B now become the centers for two arcs that establish those parts of the ellipse that occupy the acute corners of the isometric square.

4

5

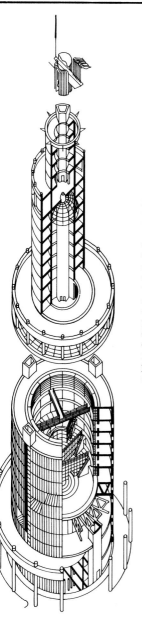

The decision to draft a cylindrical figure that involves a series of repeated circular plans usually takes the designer to the directly drafted rapidity of a plan oblique. For example, this elaborate tower structure from a drawing by Mark Goldstein was not only quick to construct, but its true-plan circle allows--after cutting away parts of the cylinder and exploding its form--a more penetrating view into its core.

How to Render Axonometrics and Isometrics

1

Due to the inherent strength of its depth illusion the axonometric is comparatively easy to render, even by those with only basic drafting skills. For example, by the singular concentration of rendering on only visible wall planes, or only on visible floor planes, or their combination, the illusion of axonometric space--quite apart from the attendant increase in information--is actually enhanced.

Axonometric and, indeed, isometric planes are quickly rendered by any one of the following mediums:

painted washes of ink, watercolor, or gouache

dry-colored "mechanically" or tinted monochromatically using dry-transfer medium

subjected to a collage of colored papers

rendered in graphite or ink as hatched areas of value or delineated to describe modules or textures of the finishes of materials

This axonometric, redrawn from the work of Haverstock Associates, uses a medium value dry-transfer screen of dots that is applied selectively to all "solid" wall planes along one axial direction only. Apart from intensifying the spatial illusion of this drawing, the transparency of this medium maintains a see-through continuity of delineated forms and fittings that occur immediately behind the rendered planes. However, to avoid a graphic clutter, the modular grids of floor finishes have not been permitted a visual contact whenever they pass behind these planes.

2

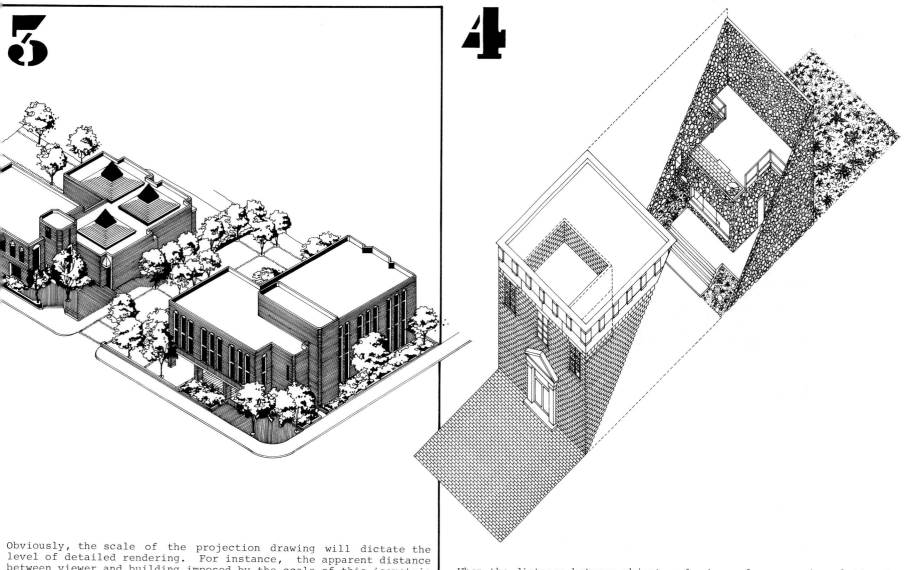

3

4

Obviously, the scale of the projection drawing will dictate the level of detailed rendering. For instance, the apparent distance between viewer and building imposed by the scale of this isometric drawing after that by the practice of Garnet, Cloughly, and Blakemore allows only a system of directional lines that imply the scaled horizontal grain of coursework on walls, pyramid roofs, and floorscape.

When the distance between object and viewer decreases in relation to the size of the form, more detail can be inserted. This expanded axonometric of a prototype design for a bank building is taken from the work of the Site group. It clearly displays the contrast between a ruled, mechanical rendition and that of a building material and groundscape more suited to freehand drawing.

The Functions of Axonometrics and Isometrics

Despite their widespread popularity, the bird-like viewpoint inherent in metric projection drawing is criticized by some designers who feel that--when they are used as design tools--they project a design stance far too unrelated to our normal perception of objects and environment. However, their real ability is as a catalyst for the preview of a three-dimensional fusion of the plan, elevation, section, and--depending on the viewing requirement--the "fifth" elevation, i.e., the roof plane.

Another function of projection drawings is as an easily understood communication vehicle. They are often used to explain events in time, such as developmental design sequences, the phased stages in the erection of a building, or, as in this trio of planometrics derived from the work of Arata Isozaki, the progressive buildup of a proposed building design from concept, via "undressed" structure, to its external impression.

By comparison to the axonometric, the lower, more realistic viewpoint of the isometric is more used for looking "at" than "into" forms. Isometrics function well as exploded or expanded graphics that communicate component assembly, such as in buildings or complicated machine parts.

Generally, the undistorted plan projection offered by the axonometric gives this graphic mode an advantage when an interior view is required.

However, this axonometric goes further because, in order to provide an unimpeded view of its interior, the side wall has been removed and the front facade detached to create a simple exploded view. This drawing is based on one by Wendy Shillam and Michael Robertson Smith.

Another version of the exploded projection drawing is sometimes applied to multilevel buildings when the volume between a stack of floor plans is stretched vertically--either with or without scaled walls--to achieve a clear view of their perpendicular relationship.

This drawing is based on the work of John Allan.

1

2

3

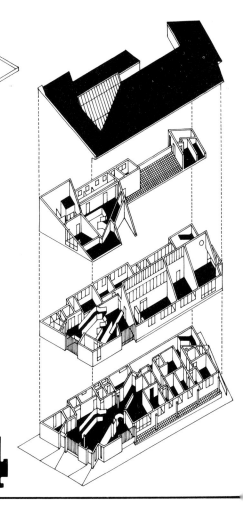

4

The Functions of Axonometrics and Isometrics

5

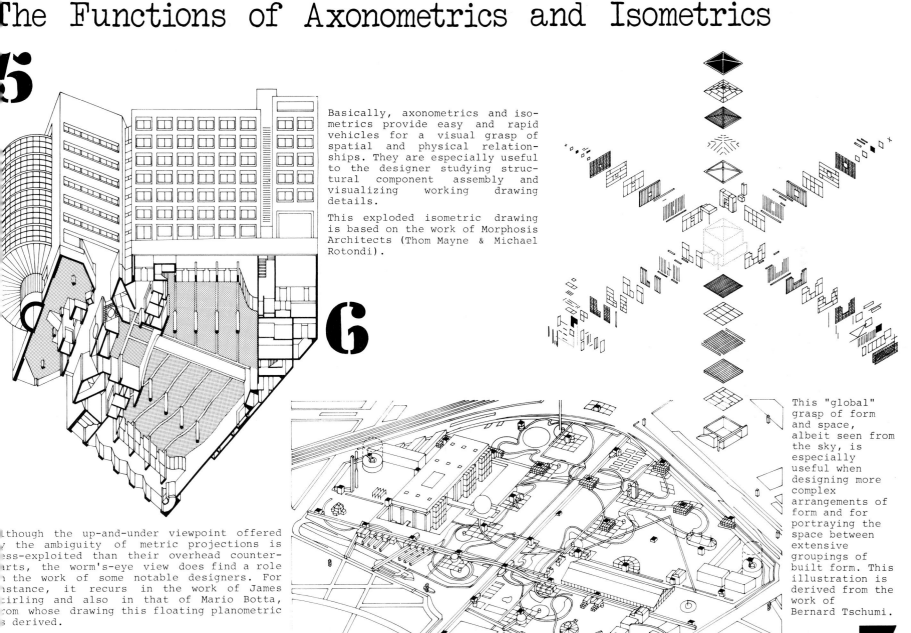

Basically, axonometrics and isometrics provide easy and rapid vehicles for a visual grasp of spatial and physical relationships. They are especially useful to the designer studying structural component assembly and visualizing working drawing details.

This exploded isometric drawing is based on the work of Morphosis Architects (Thom Mayne & Michael Rotondi).

6

Although the up-and-under viewpoint offered by the ambiguity of metric projections is less-exploited than their overhead counterparts, the worm's-eye view does find a role in the work of some notable designers. For instance, it recurs in the work of James Stirling and also in that of Mario Botta, from whose drawing this floating planometric is derived.

N.B.: Always remember that when drafting a worm's-eye projection the plan should be flipped upside down to establish the correct viewing position.

This "global" grasp of form and space, albeit seen from the sky, is especially useful when designing more complex arrangements of form and for portraying the space between extensive groupings of built form. This illustration is derived from the work of Bernard Tschumi.

7

Basic Shadow Projection in Axonometrics

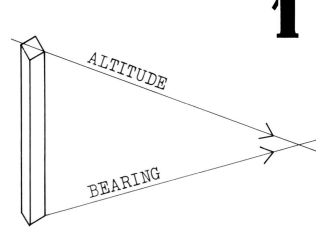

1

The length of a shadow cast from an object is found at the intersection of the two components described on page 24, namely, the plan direction of the light (azimuth, or bearing), and the angle, or altitude of the sun's rays.

2

Both of these components can be adjusted to suit the nature of the orthographic information that is to be illuminated. However, when an object is sunlit, it should be remembered that, whatever the given or assumed bearing and angle, the rays of light appear as parallel lines.

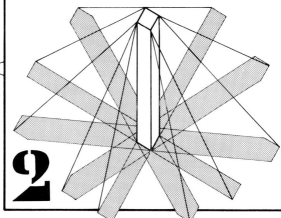

3

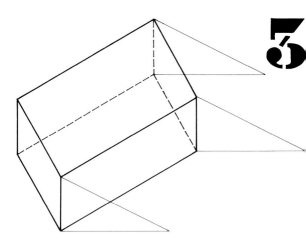

The shadow cast from a simple axonometric boxform is found by striking its shadow casting points with light rays describing the angle of altitude. The point at which this angle meets the bearing line--in this instance describing a horizontal groundplane --finds the shadow point.

4

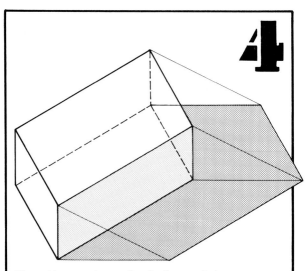

When the series of shadow points are connected, the shape of the shadow projection is completed and ready for rendering.

In architectural drawing a distinction is frequently made between the rendering of shade, i.e., the unlit areas of the surface of an illuminated object, and the shadow that is cast onto another surface from an object that intercepts light. This convention renders shade as less dark than shadow so that shaded planes can receive fenestration and other detail.

5

6

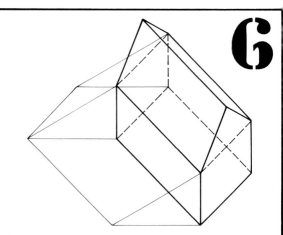

When casting shadows from slightly more complex forms, simply project each element of that form separately. For example, with an axonometric of a basic gabled house-form, first project the shadow of the "box" element.

Basic Shadow Projection in Axonometrics

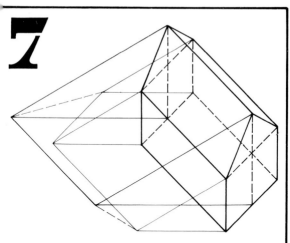

7

Then project the shadow of the gabled section of the form as an extension of the shadow already established before completing its shape by connecting all the shadow points.

Notice that the shadow points corresponding to each end of the ridge are found by bearing lines projected from points perpendicularly below them--the length of the shadow being found at their intersection with the corresponding angle of altitude.

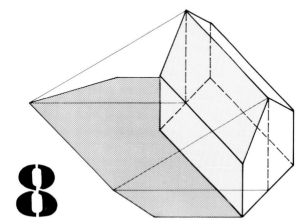

8

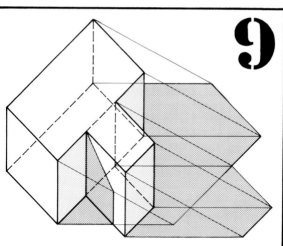

9

The same technique of separate shadow projection is used when one form projects from another, i.e., the shadow of each is projected independently to form the whole shape.

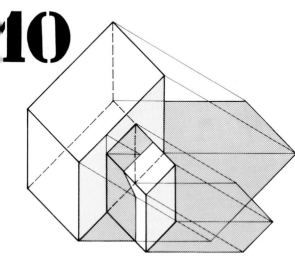

10

owever, when a projecting form occurs below he casting edge of a larger object situated etween it and the light source, the shadow f the latter will fall partly across it.

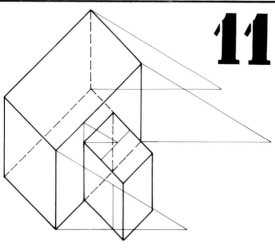

11

To find this shadow length, take any point along the casting edge of the larger form and triangulate the angle of light with that of the bearing line.

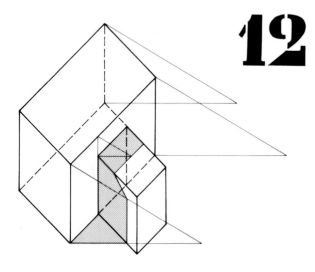

12

The resulting intersection finds the extent of the shadow line as it passes over the lower form to connect with its counterpart on the nearside plane.

Building as Center of Attention

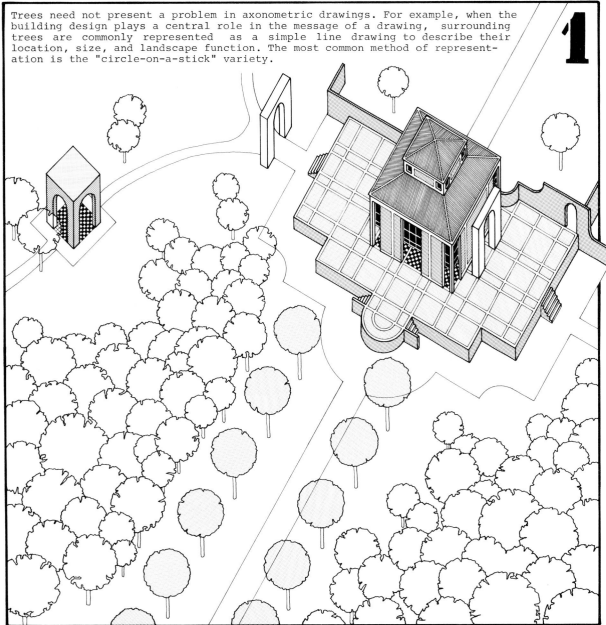

Trees need not present a problem in axonometric drawings. For example, when the building design plays a central role in the message of a drawing, surrounding trees are commonly represented as a simple line drawing to describe their location, size, and landscape function. The most common method of representation is the "circle-on-a-stick" variety.

1

These are quickly drafted from the plan to appear convincing as individual events, in groups, and when arranged into avenue formation.

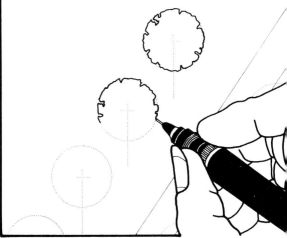

2

3 The basic "circle-on-a-stick" form is then elaborated by a meandering line that, being sensitive to the scale of the drawing, describes the soft edge of foliage.

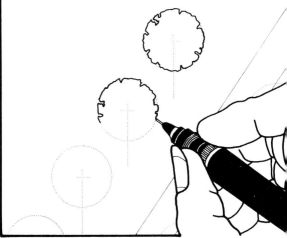

Landscape as Center of Attention

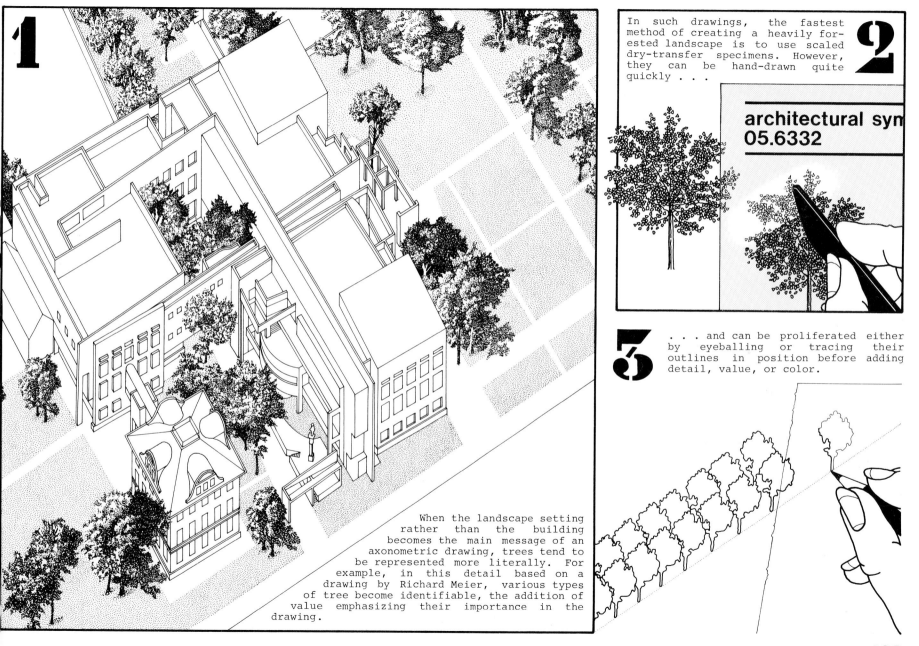

1

2 In such drawings, the fastest method of creating a heavily forested landscape is to use scaled dry-transfer specimens. However, they can be hand-drawn quite quickly . . .

architectural syn
05.6332

3 . . . and can be proliferated either by eyeballing or tracing their outlines in position before adding detail, value, or color.

When the landscape setting rather than the building becomes the main message of an axonometric drawing, trees tend to be represented more literally. For example, in this detail based on a drawing by Richard Meier, various types of tree become identifiable, the addition of value emphasizing their importance in the drawing.

Trees in Axonometrics: Wooded Areas

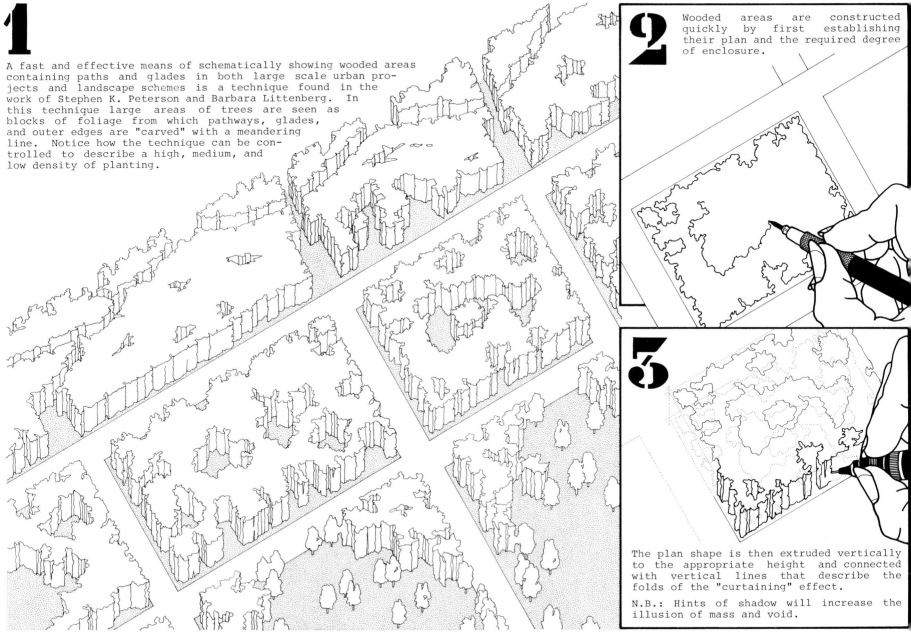

1

A fast and effective means of schematically showing wooded areas containing paths and glades in both large scale urban projects and landscape schemes is a technique found in the work of Stephen K. Peterson and Barbara Littenberg. In this technique large areas of trees are seen as blocks of foliage from which pathways, glades, and outer edges are "carved" with a meandering line. Notice how the technique can be controlled to describe a high, medium, and low density of planting.

2

Wooded areas are constructed quickly by first establishing their plan and the required degree of enclosure.

3

The plan shape is then extruded vertically to the appropriate height and connected with vertical lines that describe the folds of the "curtaining" effect.

N.B.: Hints of shadow will increase the illusion of mass and void.

5 PERSPECTIVES

Introducing Perspective

1

Perspective drawing has the advantage over all other modes of graphic representation because not only can it incorporate all the depth cues found across the range of orthographics, but it also possesses one that is denied to them, i.e., convergence.

Convergence is the diminishing effect of objects as they appear at points increasingly distant from the eye. Even when reduced graphically to a linear diagram, this spatial cue is extremely powerful when describing an illusion of depth.

Therefore, perspective represents the graphic illusion nearest to the way we perceive space and form. It is also used frequently in sketch form during design development and also as a summary of the designer's intent when communicating with clients.

2 3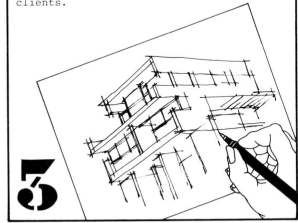

4

Because of the modern movement's preference for the model, the perspective has suffered from a demise in architectural presentation. There has also been an attendant suspicion that an artful perspective can display a design proposal in an impossibly favorable light. However, despite these setbacks, perspective remains the most potent drawing force in graphic communication. Its skill is learned in the experience of sketching--an activity that not only is improved by a basic understanding of perspective construction but also supplies immeasurable feedback to the production of presentation perspectives.

5

By offering an almost limitless choice of vantage points from which to observe an object or a three-dimensional idea, perspective frees the designer from the fixed range of viewpoints that govern orthographics.

This dynamic perspective drawing on the left is based on a painting by Iakov Chernikhov.

As the basis of one-point, or parallel, perspective has already been outlined in chapters 1, 2, and 3, and, together with two-point, or angular perspective, been covered in the previous manuals, the following nine pages describe a quick and convenient method for converting plans into an accurate perspective view using two or more vanishing points.

106

Office Method Perspective

1

This fast and accurate method of angled perspective is one that does not--like several other methods--require that the plan be tilted. It begins with the roof plan of the building fixed square-on near to the top of the drawing board.

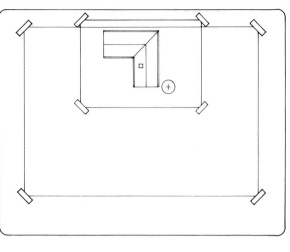

N.B.: It is a good idea to keep the referent elevation close at hand as this will act as a useful guide when tracing information.

2

Next tape a sheet of tracing paper over the plan. As the tracing paper will carry the station point and, if possible, the vanishing points, it should be considerably larger than the drawing of the plan.

3

Then trace the plan and include any surrounding details, such as trees, pathways, and so on.

4

The location of all windows and doors that will be seen in the finished perspective, together with any projections, such as balconies, piers, chimneys, and so on, should also be marked on the tracing.

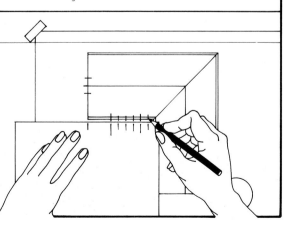

5

If the building comprises two or more storeys, then it is advisable to trace the features of each floor, or roof, in different colored pencils or inks.

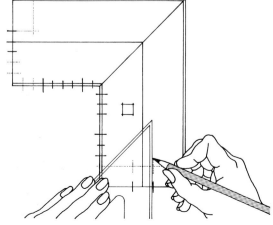

107

Establishing the Direction of View

1

The exact viewpoint from which the building will appear to the spectator when drawn should now be established. This necessitates the location of the station point, i.e., the distance between the viewer and the building.

A factor in locating the station point is the extent of the arc of vision, i.e., the angle formed by two lines that radiate from the station point to determine the extreme edges of the picture.

2

ARC OF VISION 40°

Obviously, if the spectator is standing only a few feet away from the building, the angle of vision would be so wide as to place most of the picture out of focus. Therefore, it is generally agreed that the angle of vision should not be more than 60 degrees and not less than 40 degrees.

When positioning the station point, a general rule is that the spectator should be at a distance of about three times the height of the building.

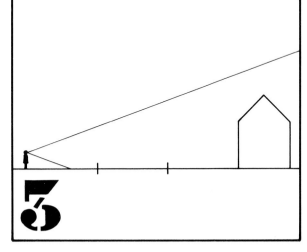

3

4

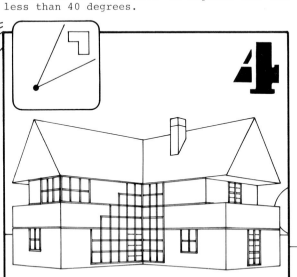

When working with square or rectangular buildings, avoid placing the spectator in a position from which a symmetrical view with equally foreshortened planes is given.

5

Aim instead for the interesting variety of two side planes with differing angles of perspective.

Establishing the Picture Plane

1

STATION POINT

Having located the station point, the next operation is to project the two lines that describe the arc of vision so that they determine the outer edges of the desired picture. Any object that falls outside these lines will not appear in the final drawing.

2

Now bisect the angle of vision. This line establishes the center of vision. It should now be obvious that the perspective image as viewed within the angle of vision must, in order to be in focus, occur on a plane that is at right angles to the center of vision.

CENTER OF VISION

3

For example, imagine a slide projector: the center of vision represents the direction in which it is beamed; the two extremity lines represent the arc of its projected rays of light. To achieve a true projected image, the screen must be at right angles to the direction in which it is pointed.

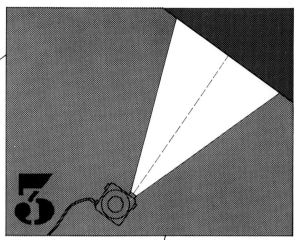

4

If we now replace the analogy of the projector screen with a plane drawn at right angles to the center of vision, we visualize the picture plane --represented on the plan by a line.

PICTURE PLANE

5

If we move this "screen," or picture plane, away from or nearer the station point, and keep it at right angles to the center of vision, we can either reduce or enlarge the image. This is an important aspect for consideration when locating the picture plane.

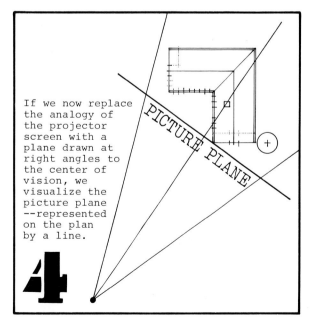

The Function of the Picture Plane

1

In this setup the line representing the picture plane has been located just in front of the plan and actually touches the near corner of the building.

However, if a larger image of the building were required, it would be necessary to position the picture plane as cutting through the plan. Sometimes it can be placed to touch a corner and provide a convenient height line.

2

3

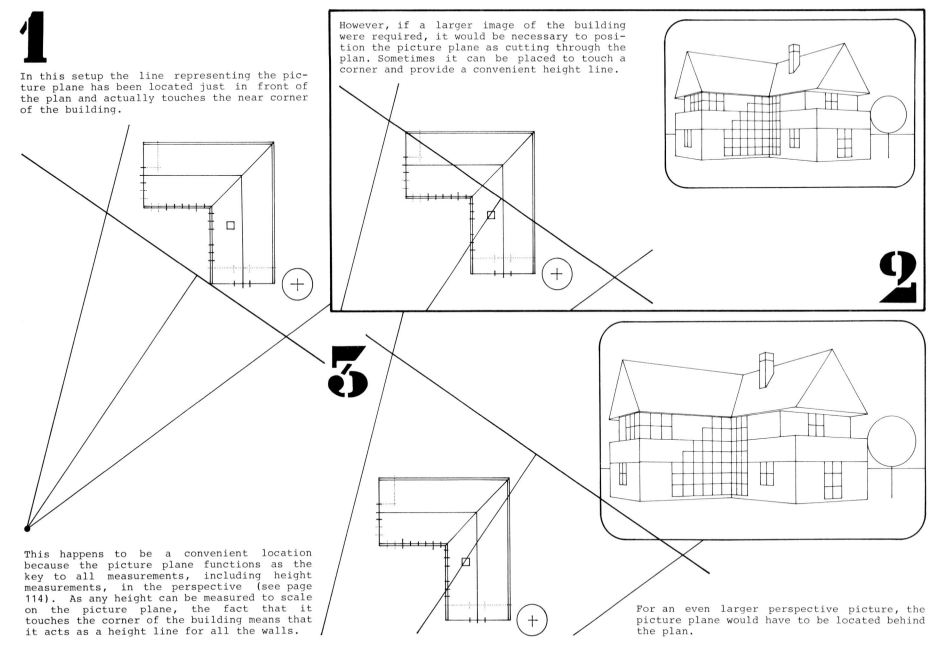

This happens to be a convenient location because the picture plane functions as the key to all measurements, including height measurements, in the perspective (see page 114). As any height can be measured to scale on the picture plane, the fact that it touches the corner of the building means that it acts as a height line for all the walls.

For an even larger perspective picture, the picture plane would have to be located behind the plan.

Establishing the Vanishing Points

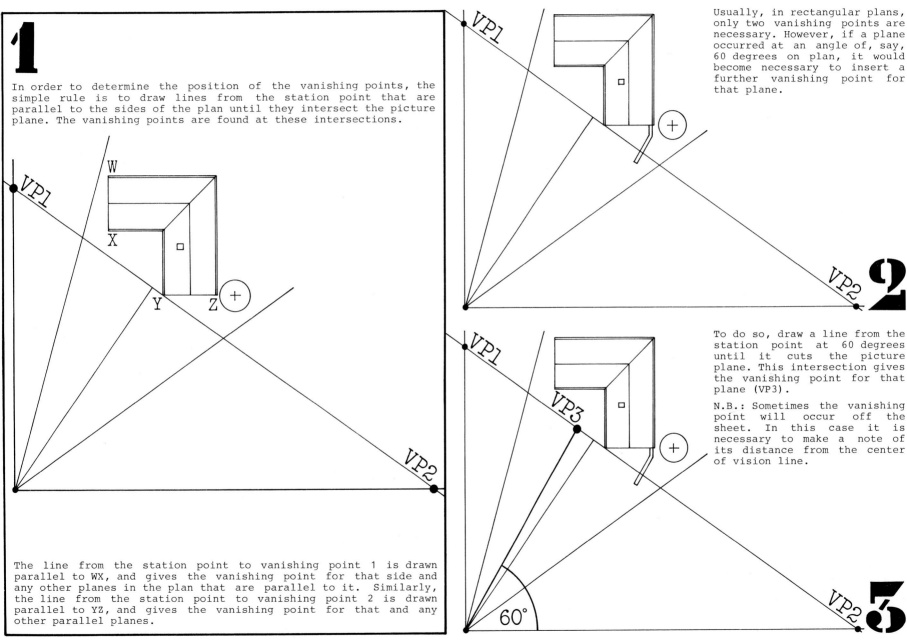

1

In order to determine the position of the vanishing points, the simple rule is to draw lines from the station point that are parallel to the sides of the plan until they intersect the picture plane. The vanishing points are found at these intersections.

The line from the station point to vanishing point 1 is drawn parallel to WX, and gives the vanishing point for that side and any other planes in the plan that are parallel to it. Similarly, the line from the station point to vanishing point 2 is drawn parallel to YZ, and gives the vanishing point for that and any other parallel planes.

2

Usually, in rectangular plans, only two vanishing points are necessary. However, if a plane occurred at an angle of, say, 60 degrees on plan, it would become necessary to insert a further vanishing point for that plane.

3

To do so, draw a line from the station point at 60 degrees until it cuts the picture plane. This intersection gives the vanishing point for that plane (VP3).

N.B.: Sometimes the vanishing point will occur off the sheet. In this case it is necessary to make a note of its distance from the center of vision line.

Establishing Heights and Widths

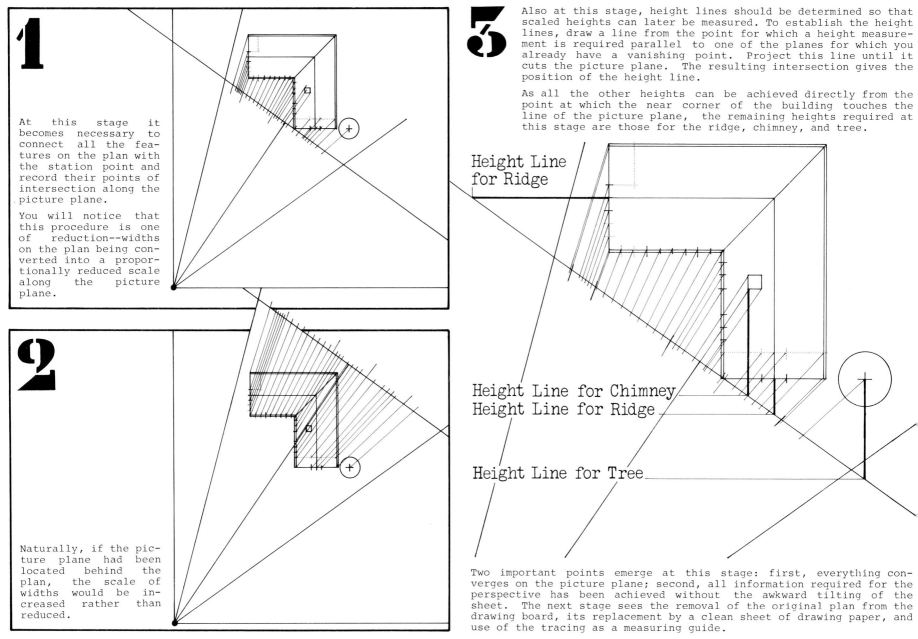

1

At this stage it becomes necessary to connect all the features on the plan with the station point and record their points of intersection along the picture plane.

You will notice that this procedure is one of reduction--widths on the plan being converted into a proportionally reduced scale along the picture plane.

2

Naturally, if the picture plane had been located behind the plan, the scale of widths would be increased rather than reduced.

3

Also at this stage, height lines should be determined so that scaled heights can later be measured. To establish the height lines, draw a line from the point for which a height measurement is required parallel to one of the planes for which you already have a vanishing point. Project this line until it cuts the picture plane. The resulting intersection gives the position of the height line.

As all the other heights can be achieved directly from the point at which the near corner of the building touches the line of the picture plane, the remaining heights required at this stage are those for the ridge, chimney, and tree.

Height Line for Ridge

Height Line for Chimney
Height Line for Ridge

Height Line for Tree

Two important points emerge at this stage: first, everything converges on the picture plane; second, all information required for the perspective has been achieved without the awkward tilting of the sheet. The next stage sees the removal of the original plan from the drawing board, its replacement by a clean sheet of drawing paper, and use of the tracing as a measuring guide.

Transferring the Perspective Coordinates

1

Remove the tracing and the original plan drawing from the drawing board and replace with a clean sheet of drawing paper.

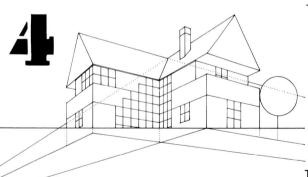

Next fold the tracing paper along the line of the picture plane, making sure that the point where the center of vision cuts the picture plane is clearly marked. This point will function as a check during the transfer of the traced measurements.

2

Now draw a horizon line across the lower part of the drawing paper. This line is the datum line for height measurements and is usually taken to be the groundline on a level site.

N.B.: Any line can represent the datum line provided that every measurement taken from it is first taken from a corresponding datum line on the elevation.

4

EYE LEVEL

On the other hand, if the ground falls away rapidly from the building, a more convincing perspective impression of the building, or group of buildings, will necessitate the lowering of the eye level below the groundline. In this event a certain amount of the form will be lost behind the rising foreground of the worm's-eye perspective view.

The next decision involves the location of the eye level, or horizon line. Normal eye level is usually 5'-6" (1650mm) or so above ground level. However, if the nature of the landscape is to feature in the final drawing, or a more general view of a group of buildings is required, it would be necessary to raise the eye level. For example, a bird's-eye view is achieved when the level is elevated to a height of 30 or 40 feet above the groundline.

EYE LEVEL

3

In any event, whether the eye level is placed above or below the groundline, its ultimate location does not affect the system of working. However, a golden rule is to avoid placing the eye level line at the same height as any significant horizontal line on the building, such as the eaves or other projection. This is because it will exist simply as a line in the finished perspective and thus lose its sense of projection.

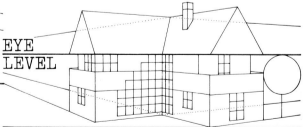

EYE
LEVEL

5

Setting up the Perspective Drawing

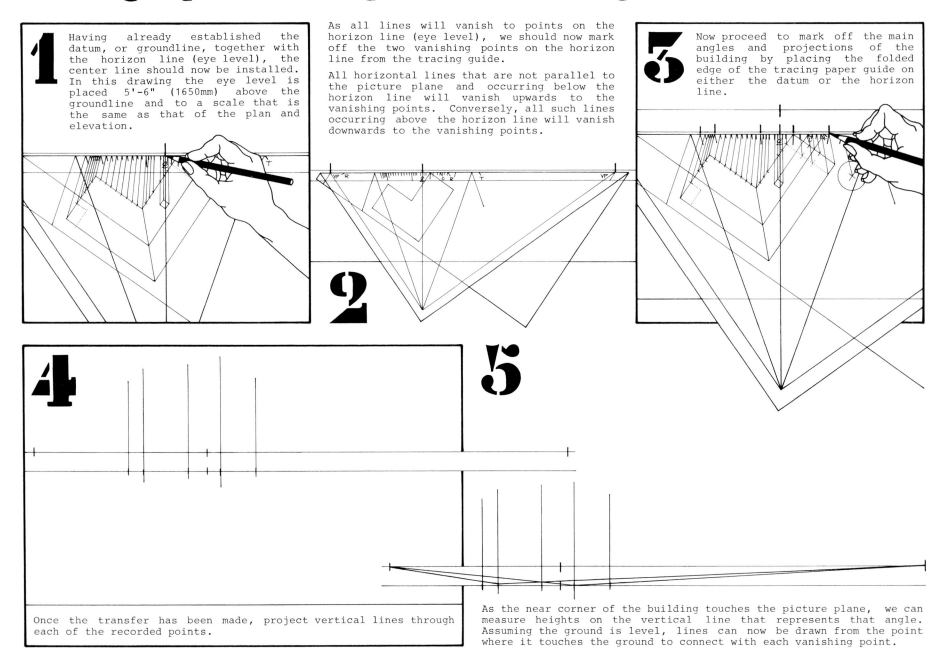

1 Having already established the datum, or groundline, together with the horizon line (eye level), the center line should now be installed. In this drawing the eye level is placed 5'-6" (1650mm) above the groundline and to a scale that is the same as that of the plan and elevation.

2 As all lines will vanish to points on the horizon line (eye level), we should now mark off the two vanishing points on the horizon line from the tracing guide.

All horizontal lines that are not parallel to the picture plane and occurring below the horizon line will vanish upwards to the vanishing points. Conversely, all such lines occurring above the horizon line will vanish downwards to the vanishing points.

3 Now proceed to mark off the main angles and projections of the building by placing the folded edge of the tracing paper guide on either the datum or the horizon line.

4 Once the transfer has been made, project vertical lines through each of the recorded points.

5 As the near corner of the building touches the picture plane, we can measure heights on the vertical line that represents that angle. Assuming the ground is level, lines can now be drawn from the point where it touches the ground to connect with each vanishing point.

Setting up the Perspective Drawing

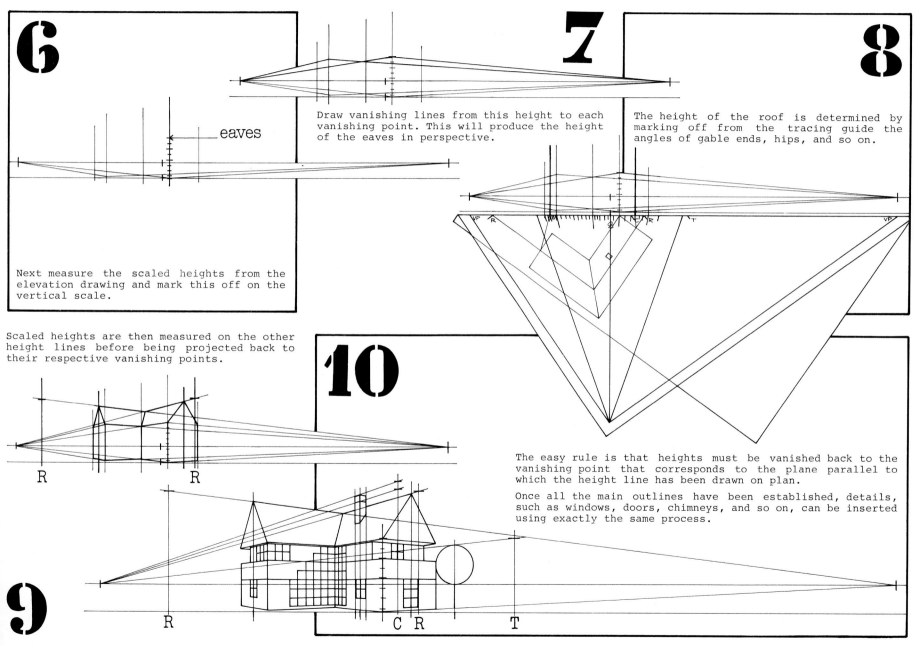

6

eaves

Next measure the scaled heights from the elevation drawing and mark this off on the vertical scale.

Scaled heights are then measured on the other height lines before being projected back to their respective vanishing points.

7

Draw vanishing lines from this height to each vanishing point. This will produce the height of the eaves in perspective.

8

The height of the roof is determined by marking off from the tracing guide the angles of gable ends, hips, and so on.

10

The easy rule is that heights must be vanished back to the vanishing point that corresponds to the plane parallel to which the height line has been drawn on plan.

Once all the main outlines have been established, details, such as windows, doors, chimneys, and so on, can be inserted using exactly the same process.

9

Adding Groups of Figures in Perspectives

1 If groups of figures are required, their size must be true to the scale of the building. This is easily done using the same method as before. First determine the position of the group on the plan.

2 Then, on plan, take a line parallel to one of the planes for which you have vanishing points, from the group to the picture plane. This gives the height line.

Now draw a line on plan from the station point through the group to the picture plane. This gives the vertical position of the group when marked off in perspective. **3**

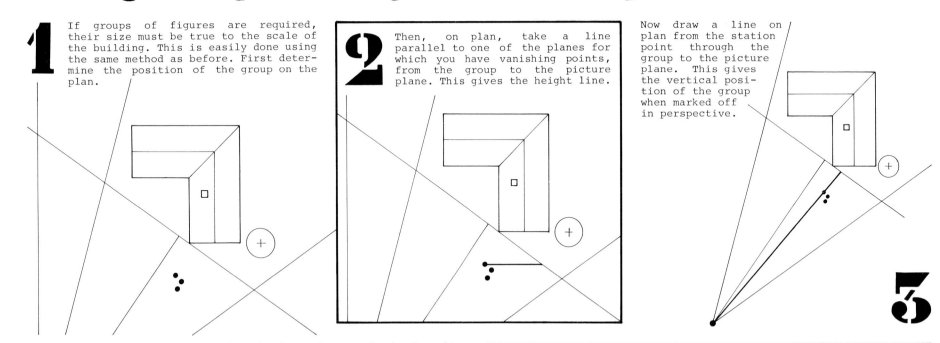

If the eye level is 6'-0" (1800mm) above datum, the horizon line can be taken as an approximation of the height of a person. Therefore, if a line is drawn from the proper vertical plane and through the height line at ground level until it cuts the vertical position of the group, the correct perspective height is achieved.

In fact, anywhere between this point and the height line, the group will be true to scale and in perspective.

N.B.: As figures are used as an important scale attribute, and as they often appear in the foreground, it is important to use a reference aid when drawing them.

EYE LEVEL   VERTICAL POSITION OF GROUP   HEIGHT LINE   VP

DATUM

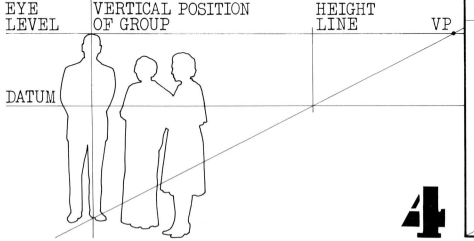

4

5

The Function of Trees in Perspectives

1 By contrast to the insertion of trees in dimensionless space of elevations, those in the apparent three dimensions of a perspective can be used to intensify the spatial illusion. For example, trees can appear to emphasize the presence of space between picture plane and middleground, and also define the space between message area and background. Drawing based on the work of Roger Huntley.

It is possible to develop one's own style and technique for creating canopies of foliage that, in framing the buildings, both channel the view to the message area and filter glimpses through to less important zones of the drawing.

2

3 Another function of trees in perspectives is to temper the mechanical starkness of their construction. This softening effect is often used by illustrators who will graphically "plant" shrubs or trees in front of more aggressive or acute angles in the drawing (after Archives d'Architecture Moderne).

4 Therefore, the best way of approaching the use of trees in perspective is as a pictorial counter-balance. They should be included both as a foil to the geometry of the perspective, and as a compositional means of adjusting the picture's center of gravity.

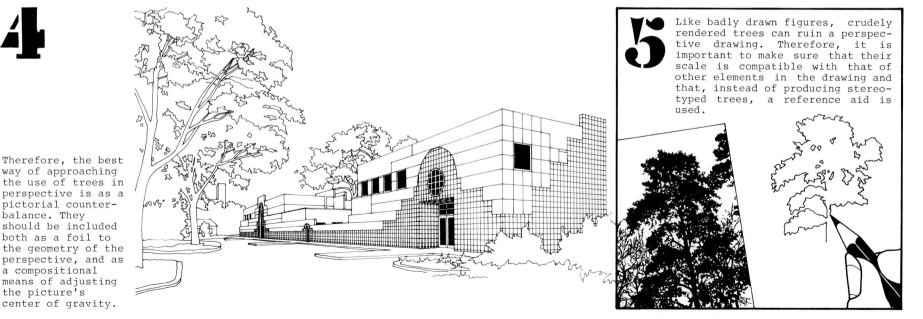

5 Like badly drawn figures, crudely rendered trees can ruin a perspective drawing. Therefore, it is important to make sure that their scale is compatible with that of other elements in the drawing and that, instead of producing stereotyped trees, a reference aid is used.

Composing Perspective Drawings

1 Before rendering a perspective drawing, a key decision will affect the positioning of the outer edges of the graphic format, i.e., the location of the frame of reference. This decision is linked to the degree of emphasis that is to be given to the three pictorial zones: foreground, middleground, and background.

For instance, if both background and foreground are composed of equal areas in the drawing, the result will tend to appear commonplace and visually tame.

2 Therefore, in order to design a more telling composition it is important that emphasis be given to either the background zone or to the foreground zone. Drawing based on the work of Dominic Michaelis Associates.

3 If the landscape format is upended into the vertical prominence of the portrait format, a strong feeling of overhead space is induced when we place a more dominant emphasis on the sky area--and with it the need for some elaboration of that zone.

4 Conversely, if the foreground area represents an important feature of the design, then the increased emphasis of this pictorial area may bring the attendant need for a more considered and detailed rendering; as this zone occurs nearest to the viewer.

N.B.: In each case, the point of the drawing, i.e., the building design, remains as the central focus of the composition.

Composing Perspective Drawings

5

A further decision that strongly affects both the compositional impact of the drawing and its message is the infusion of light, shade, and shadow, and its direction.

For example, the building forms can be generally illuminated from the left . . .

6 . . . or from the right. The chosen direction will correspond to those planes whose detail you wish to communicate.

7

A further exploitation of compositional patterning is the use of a tonal contrast that recognizes the outline of the parts of the buildings in shade or shadow as silhouetted against the light areas of the background. Conversely, the lighter portions of the buildings' outline mass can be intensified by a contrast with adjacent dark background areas. These illustrations are developed from a line drawing by Allies and Morrison.

Through a deliberate handling of the compositional dimensions of light and contrast together with their relationship to the location of the picture's frame, or window, various optional compositions may be explored. These are best studied using thumbnail sketches before rendering the one that appears to convey the most potent image of the buildings and their setting.

8

Rendering Perspective Drawings

1

An accurately constructed and well-composed perspective delineation is only the first stage in the production of a quality drawing. It is the ensuing rendering stage that transforms the mechanical coldness of construction lines into a picture imbued with light, atmosphere, and quality of surface. However, being inhibited by the geometry of perspective construction, some students find it difficult to make this transition and will often allow its mechanical bleakness to communicate their designs. Therefore, the best way of approaching the rendering stage is to employ the construction drawing simply for what it is, i.e., merely a basic framework to guide the application treatment of the medium of your choice.

To avoid intimidation by the construction drawing, many designers will render onto a tracing paper overlay. This method separates the two stages and allows a singular concentration on the rendering technique that is applied against the guideline underlay--the latter being later discarded. Another tracing paper method sees the construction worked in nonrepro blue pencil, the final rendition being overworked in ink for a diazo print.

2

However, a perspective drawing can exist simply as a linear event but, in this case, what is left out of the drawing is as important as that which is retained. It is the concentration on line quality, selectivity, and emphasis that can separate a labored drawing with a "wooden" appearance from the sheer elegance of one such as this, based on the work of Richard Rogers and Partners.

3

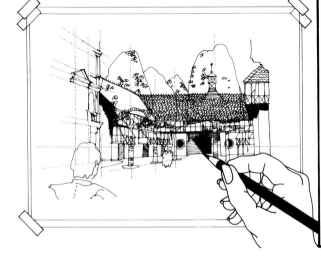

This more formally composed perspective is based on the work of Franco Purini and Laura Thermes. It illustrates the selective application of a simple but effective rendering technique to target a contrast of materials, shade, and shadow. Notice that the foliage treatment contrasts with the more directional use of tone elsewhere and that, also by contrast, it both compliments and strengthens the impact of that part of the skyline.

Rendering Perspective Drawings

Here are two perspective drawings taken from the work of Christopher and Elspeth Cross. They demonstrate a more relaxed version of supportive tonal hatching that is applied minimally to selected areas of shade and shadow in the space of the perspectives. Having the quality of a quick sketch, they impart the "I was there" feeling, even though their spaces existed only in the mind's eye of the designer. Notice that the shading, rather than appearing as an appendage, occurs as a natural extension of the line drawing.

4

5

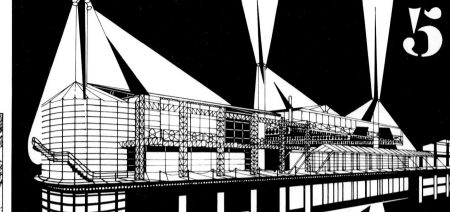

In stark contrast is this detail from a nighttime view of a pier design redrawn from the work of Alsop and Lyall. Here, line and solid tone combine to etch a powerful impression of the architectural form --a quality that is characteristic of the graphics of this practice. An analysis of this drawing discovers a deliberate transformation of its perspective framework into a simple, bold image that conveys drama and demands attention.

6

This drawing uses two rendering treatments to exploit the difference between the view of a city avenue and a proposed rapid transit station. By contrasting the delineation of the station design with a heavier treatment of existing buildings and trees, the eye is drawn to the subjective form in the drawing but, at the same time, retaining the integrity of a contextual relationship.

7

An important aspect of perspectives drawn of forms that, hitherto, existed only in the space of an idea is that of scale. The sense of scale imparted by a drawing is governed by its author's ability to indicate correctly and selectively the modular and textural surfaces of its planes together with familiar objects and people. For example, this drawing--from one produced by Chapman Taylor Associates--is saturated with clues as to its scale. Here, the rendering technique focuses almost exclusively on surface quality and the modular size of its components. In so doing, it creates a kind of richness so often lacking in many other drawings of this genre.

Interior Perspectives Using Site Photographs

1 A very simple method of producing a perspective image that conveys the relationship between inside and outside space is to incorporate photographs taken on-site into a basic outline drawing. This is a technique much used by architects, including Mies van der Rohe on whose work this illustration is based. The technique relies upon taking on-site photographs of views as they would be seen from the area of the proposed building. The photographs should then be processed as color or monochrome prints.

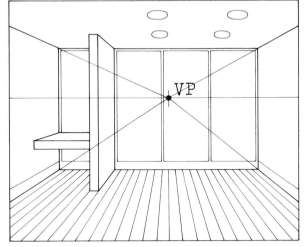

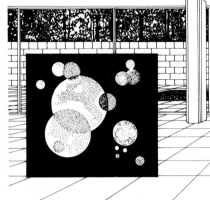

2 A single point interior perspective is constructed in outline with a vanishing point that coincides with a point on or near to any major glazed connection with outside space.

3 This can then be ink-drawn before cropping the appropriate photograph to fit the shape of the view as defined by the window or glazed aperture.

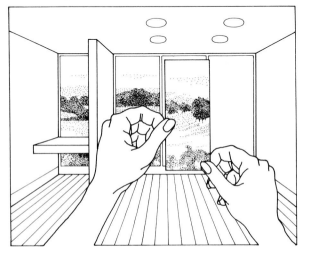

4 When the photograph is glued or heat-sealed into position, the result is a convincing image. Its effect is extended by the insertion of selected surface finishes and the addition of trace-cut figures found in magazines.

5

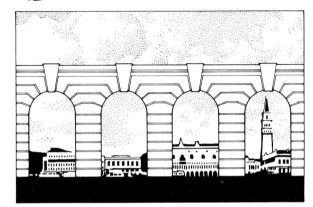

There are many uses for this technique, such as in interior wall elevations or, indeed, any drawing that relates layers of architectural space with an existing setting.

Perspectives Using Diazo Prints

1

In Manual of Graphic Techniques 1 we described a technique for printing an enlarged image from a 35mm slide using the diazo process. This involved the use of an unexposed sheet of diazo print paper as a screen onto which a slide is projected in a darkened room for an exposure of between 30 and 40 minutes. When using the semi-dry diazo process, "normal" print paper should be used; when using the ammonia diazo process, use black-line, blue-line, etc.

However, quite apart from the enlargement facility of this technique, diazo printing slide photographs has proved itself to be a very useful design tool, especially when used as the basis of a perspective of a design proposal shown directly in relation to its setting.

First, aim a projector loaded with the focused slide at the diazo print paper "screen." The slide used should result from a site photograph taken from a position that provides the best vantage point from which to view the building.

2

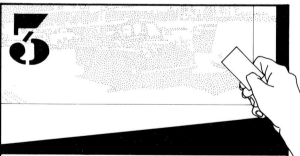

3

Remember that the larger the projected image, the greater the length of exposure. One method of checking the progress of the exposure is to quickly switch the room light on and off. An alternative method of monitoring the exposure is to hold a piece of already exposed diazo print paper against the "screen." As the yellow of unexposed diazo print paper turns white when fully exposed, this color-matching check can be made in the light of the projector beam.

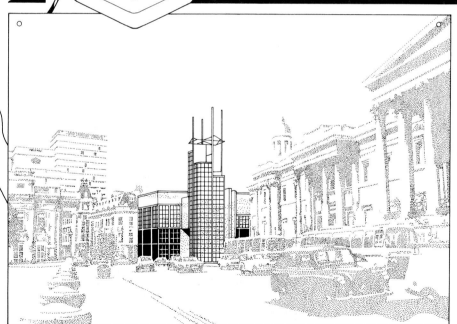

4

When the exposure process is finished, protect the light-sensitive print surface until developing by diazo in the normal way. The resultant print can now function as the setting in which a colored ink drawing of the building design can be made--its perspective coordinates being governed by those of the photographic print.

The building shown in this illustration is based on a design by Ahrends, Burton, and Koralek.

123

Traced Perspectives from Photographic Prints

Photographs are useful as sources for perspective drawings, especially when presenting "before" and "after" impressions of modifications to an existing architecture. First find the horizon line (eye level) by aligning a ruler against the edge of all receding planes, such as window sills, that appear as horizontal in the photograph and mark this in the margin to either side of the print.

Now tape the print to the drawing board and overlay this with a taped sheet of tracing paper.

1

Using a pencil, extend the horizon line across the overlay and, with reference to the existing building, project the main lines of convergence to find the vanishing points. If the vanishing points occur off the overlay, simply mark these onto a strip of masking tape fixed into position on the board.

2

Trace the main outlines of the existing building, leaving the approximate area that will be occupied by the architectural addition. All areas of the existing building that will appear in the final drawing can be confidently detailed at this stage.

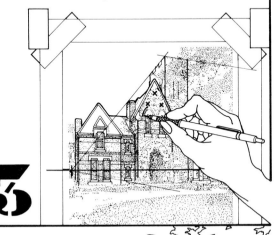

3

Next slip a sheet of white paper between the tracing and the print. Using the perspective coordinates established from the photograph, project the outlines of the addition using proportional cues, such as the size of doors and the modules of building materials, to establish its scale in relation to the existing form. The addition can now be detailed in the manner used for recording the existing building.

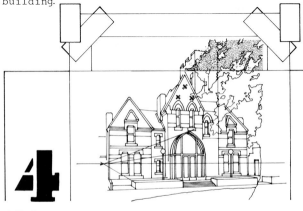

4

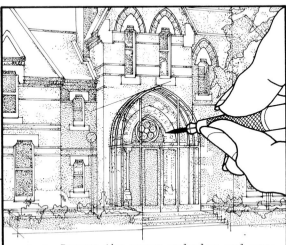

5 Remove the paper underlay and complete the drawing by inserting any detail of the existing building that may be seen through the new addition.

The pencil tracing can be directly converted into an ink-drawn perspective or be used as an underlay for a second-stage rendition.

6

Composite Photographs from Models and Slides

1 The photographed combination of a model against its intended setting represented by a projected 35mm slide of the site can produce an exciting perspective preview of a building design both for its designer and for the client. The setup is basic. First place the model on a table in front of a large projection screen, or a backdrop of white paper, or a white painted wall. Then tape a sheet of folded white paper to the top of the table so that its large side drapes over the front facing the projector.

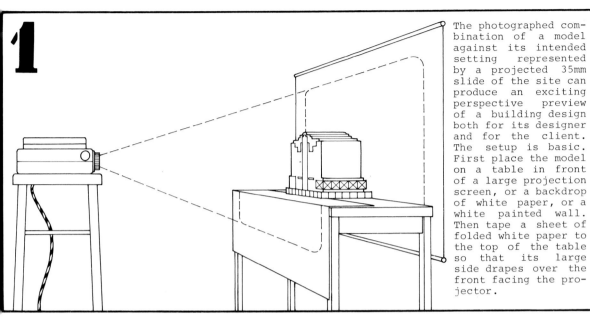

4 Here are two prints made from 35mm color slides using the technique described here. The three-dimensional quality of the model appears to survive being "washed" by the front-projected slide image and, in the lower example, "foreground" information seems separated from "background" information. This layered effect results from the positioning of the two screens--one picking up the projection forward of the model and the other picking up the image behind the model. The slides were taken by Sonny Ching, a sixth-year architecture student, using a 1 : 200 scale model of his design for a Computer Research and Development Center sited hypothetically in Hong Kong.

2 Insert the site slide into the projector and beam its image at the model, backdrop, and foreground white paper screen. Maneuver both projector and model until the scale and positioning of the model and the beamed image are synchronized.

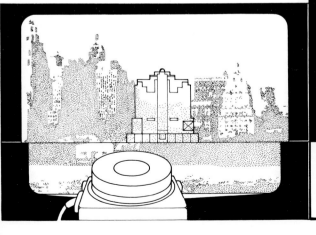

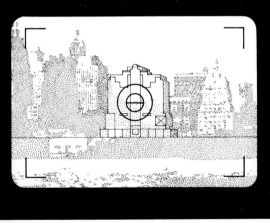

3 The combined model-slide image can now be photographed in a darkened room using a camera with a macro lens and fitted to a tripod for a long exposure.

Panoramic Perspectives from Projected Slides

1

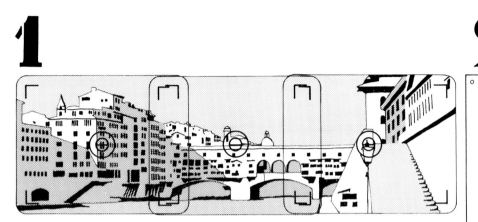

The easiest shortcut to producing perspective drawings of existing spaces is via the tracing of projected photographic prints or slides onto a "screen" of drawing paper.

A development of this technique is the panoramic perspective derived from two or more projected sections. For this technique the original photographs should be taken with care, each shot in the sequence allowing some overlap so that, at the drawing stage, the second and third projected slide can readily be connected to the drawn sections.

2 After pinning the drawing paper to the wall, the first slide is inserted into the projector and its projected image adjusted so that it corresponds to its allocated size and location on the drawing paper.

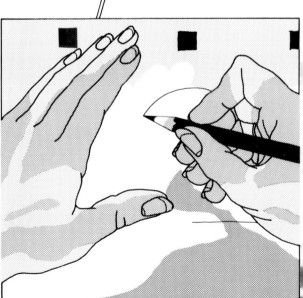

N.B.: When using prints rather than slides for this technique, an opaque projector should be used.

3 The drawing is then built up section by section by tracing each projected image in turn. Between each drawing the position of the projector is adjusted so that each subsequent slide in the panoramic series is locked onto the end of the corresponding drawn section.

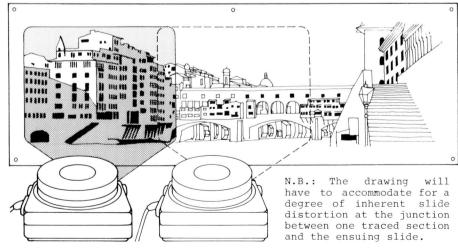

N.B.: The drawing will have to accommodate for a degree of inherent slide distortion at the junction between one traced section and the ensuing slide.

4

Discrimination of the traced line in the beam of the projected slide image can often prove difficult during the drawing stage. However, a good tip is to periodically intercept that part of the beamed image being drawn by placing the hand forward of the drawing paper. This action "removes" the projected image and allows a direct check on the progress of the drawing.

Panoramic Perspectives from Projected Slides

5 When drawing in the beam from projected slides, two basic approaches can be made. One approach is to simply produce a trace-drawing that selectively delineates the main outlines of space and form. Such drawings can be worked in pencil, fiber-tipped pen, or technical pen, and are useful when communicating site analyses.

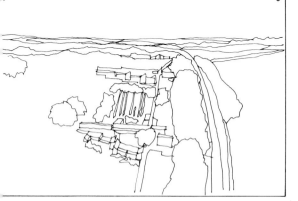

6 A tonal version can also be extracted. However, a more convincing rendering is achieved when the areas of value are structured into an open system of directional tone (see pages 40-41) so that visual contact with the projected image is maintained. It is always wise to translate the projected image into the kind of drawing dictated by its ultimate purpose in communication. This drawing represents two interpretations of the same image. The section on the right is as equally effective as its counterpart but its selectivity of detail corresponds to a drastic reduction in the amount of time spent in drawing.

7

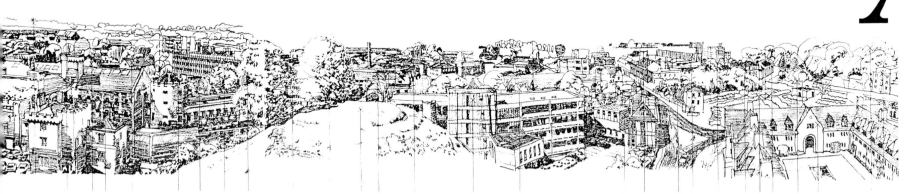

This perspective pencil drawing was produced using the slide projector method. Its author, John Cadell, a first-year architecture student, "assembled" the drawing from right to left using three source slides. Its roofscape detail was traced meticulously using a combination of silhouette line and simple hatching to translate each successive slide into drawn areas of form and value. Handwritten notes were then added above and below the drawing to develop the issues of a project that studied urban use along a stretch of the River Thames at Oxford. Although this example of the technique was produced on two sheets of A2 size paper (approximately half imperial), there is no limit to the size of a projected image. For example, wall painters often project slides of mural designs onto the sides of large buildings as a means of transferring and rescaling accurately their outlines before painting.

Index